BREAKING
FINANCIAL CURSES

BREAKING FINANCIAL CURSES

LIVING AN ABUNDANT LIFE

Spiritual Warfare Series
Volume 7

Nellie Odhuno-Shani

CONTENTS

DEDICATION

This book is dedicated to Jesus Christ of Nazareth, the Son of the Living God! A Husband to the widow, and Father to the fatherless. To the **Lord Jesus Christ,** our Savior, the Lion of the tribe of Judah, the Rock Of Ages, the Ancient of Days, Alpha and Omega, the Lamb who was slain, the Giver of Life, the Majestic One, Commander of the hosts of the armies of heaven, the Rose of Sharon, the Lily of The Valley, the Bright Morning Star, Emmanuel, Immortal, Invisible, Omnipotent, Omniscient, the only Wise God, Who was, Who is, Who is to come, our Help in times of trouble, our Healer, our Provider, our Deliverer, our Comforter, the Way, the Truth, the Life, demons tremble before Him, angels bow before Him, who alone is worthy to be praised!

Introduction

As we look at the Bible God is portrayed as generous towards His children, and has created silver and gold for them to enjoy. His generosity is driven by His love, and as a loving and generous God He is not in lack and says, "*All the silver and gold is mine.*" When God was creating the silver and gold, He did not create it for Satan and his allies. He created it for His children. Every time God called a person, He made him prosperous. We see this clearly in the examples of Abraham, Isaac, Jacob, King David, Solomon, and the Proverbs 31 woman, just to name a few.

God has no problem with prosperity. Although a lot of people think that poverty is humility, it is not. In fact, 2 Corinthians 8:9 says, "***For you know the grace of our Lord Jesus Christ, that though he was rich, yet for your sakes he became poor, so that you through his poverty you might become rich.***" However we have twisted it so that it sounds like, Jesus Christ became poor to set us an example. That could not be farther from the truth. He became poor so that by His poverty we might become rich – Hallelujah!

"Rich" is not only money as many people think. Prosperity is wholistic. Money is just a part of it. You can have a lot of money, but if you are constantly sick, you are not prosperous. If you have no friends and are lonely, you are not prosperous. We need to look at prosperity in its right perspective.

The Bible says that the **love of money** is the root of all evil. While we are not supposed to love money, silver and gold was created for us - believers in Jesus Christ - to bring abundance into our lives. Jesus said that He came so that we may have abundant life. Abundance is not going to bed hungry, or not being able to pay for my children's education, or not having house -rent. Abundance is, being amply supplied for by my heavenly Father in every area of my life! 2 Corinthians 9:8 says, *"And God is able to make all grace abound to you, so that in all things at all times, having all that you need, you will abound in every good work."* Prosperity is having all that I need. In all things, at all times, and abounding in every good work."

Since it is God's desire to give generously to His children, why are so many of His children languishing in poverty? This book attempts to identify some of the barriers that may be standing in the way of many well-meaning and diligent Christians. The proof of this, is the sudden prosperity I have witnessed in the lives of Christians counselled and prayed for through my ministry to break the spiritual barriers blocking their God-given prosperity.

Author

THE HEART OF GOD

A very smartly dressed lady walked into my office for a counseling session. She exuded confidence and joy, and so it came as a great surprise to me when the first thing she did was reach for tissues to wipe the now fast- flowing tears that started before she even opened her mouth.

"I cannot continue like this. God has to do something about my financial situation. I have prayed enough. I do not know what more God wants me to do! I have fasted enough. I even promised God that if He gives me money I would support the church. People are constantly stealing from me. There is no business that I start which ever succeeds. Just when I am about to get a breakthrough, my business collapses. I keep avoiding my friends because I owe them money. I keep promising to pay them but right now I am living from hand to mouth! I know that God does not want me to be rich, but all I am asking is for enough money to meet my needs."

Janice (not her real name) told me that a friend had told her to go for counseling because her situation did not make sense. She had a well-paying job yet she was constantly in debt and could not meet all her financial obligations at the end of every month. It was obvious that Janice was very frustrated and angry, and her anger was directed at God who she now saw as uncaring.

Not everyone who has come for counselling has been in as dire need as Janice. It has however become obvious that a majority of believers in Christ cannot boldly say that they have all that they need.

To the curious onlooker this common trend among Christians makes God look bad!

It makes God look like a Being who does not care about the needs of His children and who enjoys to see His children suffering - Perhaps to teach them some valuable lessons about life.

What does the Bible have to say about prosperity? Should a Christian be rich? Aren't there valuable lessons that a Christian can learn from poverty, lack and struggle? I believe that God has revealed to us His heart concerning prosperity in the Bible.

THE PROSPERITY GOSPEL

The "Prosperity Gospel" is a title that has been coined within Christian circles to describe any Gospel that teaches that God's main aim for the Christian is to be rich and very wealthy. It teaches that we can "name and claim" anything that we want from God and it will be given to us. Poverty is looked down upon as lack of faith and the congregants are encouraged to ask God for big houses, Mercedes Benzes, and lots of property. The "Prosperity Gospel" preachers have used themselves as live examples, telling their flock to see how God has blessed them (pastors) so that they too can be blessed. Most congregations do not realize that it is not rocket science to figure out how their leaders have enriched themselves. It is their offering, tithes and generous giving that has enabled their leaders to be able to afford the high-class living that they enjoy. While the pastor lives this exorbitant life style, he or she encourages the Believers to give more and more to God, so that God can bless them. I once sat in a congregation where the Pastor asked for four different types of offerings – tithes, freewill offerings, first fruits offering, and an offering for the guest speaker! My heart broke as the offering baskets were passed around four times while guilty-looking children of God kept digging into their pockets to find something that they could drop in the offering basket lest God strike them with poverty! Luke 6:38 *"Give and it will be given to you. A good measure, pressed down, shaken together and running over, will be poured into your lap. For with the measure you use, it will be measured to you"*, was gently whispered into the microphone as soft music was played in the background. Should people give in church? Yes they should. 2 Corinthians 9:6 says, *"Remember this: Whoever sows sparingly will also reap sparingly, and whoever sows generously will also reap generously."* This is a principle that runs through Scripture, that God wants us to be givers. However, how does God want us to give? I believe that we find the answer in 2 Corinthians 9:7 *"Each man should give what he has decided in his heart to give, not reluctantly or under compulsion, for God loves a cheerful giver."* This verse is saying that a Pastor must never force people to give using gimmicks to make them feel guilty! It is common to hear many Pastors say while trying to get money out of people, "Today God wants to show grace to certain people. 5 is the number of grace. So if you were born on the fifth, fifteenth, twenty- fifth or you are fifty and above but younger than sixty, this is your day. Come forward and give your best offering!" This is wrong and truth must be told.

Paul went on to tell the Corinthians after encouraging them to give generously as they had made up their minds in 2 Corinthians 9:8, *"And God is able to make all grace abound to you, so that in all things at all times, having all that you need, you will abound in every good work."* Here God is promising the giver that grace will abound to them. That means that they will experience undeserved favor. God goes on to promise that in all things and at all times, you will always have all that you need. The end result of the blessings from God is that you will abound in every good work. Meaning that wherever there is a good work to be done, you will be able to give out of your abundance. Paul further sums it up by saying in 2 Corinthians 9:11, "**You will be made rich in every way so that you can be generous on every occasion, and through us your generosity will result in thanksgiving to God.**" – Praise the Lord!

Our generosity should result in thanks giving to God! Should God choose to give me a bigger house or a better car I will give Him thanks, but that should not be my focus. Matthew 6:32-33 says, "**For the pagans run after all these things, and your heavenly Father knows that you need them. But seek first his kingdom and his righteousness, and all these things will be given to you as well.**" What are the things that the pagans run after? – The big house, nice car and high living. Are these things bad in themselves? No! This verse is telling us that our heavenly Father knows that we need these things. However we are not to seek for them. We are to seek the kingdom of God and as we do that, God will give to us the things that the pagans seek after as well.

Let me conclude here by saying that for every counterfeit, there is an original. So the counterfeit "Prosperity Gospel" has an original and true prosperity Gospel. I believe that the true Gospel of Christ is a prosperity Gospel! Whenever God called a person to serve Him, He made him prosper. Unfortunately the fake "Prosperity Gospel", has turned away many Christians from the true prosperity Gospel, hence they have "Thrown away the baby with the bath water."

GOD WANTS YOU TO PROSPER

God's heart is one of love. He sent His Son Jesus Christ to die for us on the Cross of Calvary because He loved the world. God's love for us is the motivating factor in causing us to prosper. God wants us to prosper in our finances, our health and our relationships. Unfortunately like Janice who came to see me, there are many Christians who believe the lies that have kept them living a life of poverty, lack, and struggling. Let me mention just two.

1. Poverty can be a tool that God is using in my life to teach me something good.

When we see a hungry-looking child, wearing torn clothes and worn out shoes, walking on the road on a cold and misty day, do we ever think that their parents are trying to teach them something good through poverty? How do you think God feels when He sees His children in such a state? It is no wonder that Jesus said in Matthew 7:11, *"If you, then, though you are evil, know how to give good gifts to your children, how much more will your Father in heaven give good gifts to those who ask him?"* Here Jesus is imploring us to see how ridiculous it is to think that God will give bad gifts to His children. He is saying that us who are evil still give good gifts to our children, and that He who is righteous will give even more and better gifts to His children.

When I cannot pay my rent, cannot adequately feed myself and my children, and when my child dies because I could not afford to take him or her to hospital, it pains God's loving heart.

2. Being rich gives a wrong impression.

Many Christians equate poverty with humility and being rich with being a sinner. There is nothing further from the truth. I personally have met some rich people who are very humble and generous, and some poor people who are very proud and stingy.

I was once teaching, and asked my audience if they would accept an offer for a friend to bring them to the meeting in a helicopter and drop them just outside the door. Not a single person said they would accept the offer. Why? It would give the wrong impression. Surprisingly many Christians do not want to be associated with being rich. In our "humble" prayers we ask God to give us just what we need and we see anything extra as extravagance. If God wanted us to have just what we needed and no more, He would not have told us in Luke 6:38, *"Give and it will be given to you. A good measure, pressed down, shaken together and running over will be poured into your lap."* Here we see that God wants to give until it is running over! If everything that God gives is for our own personal consumption, why would He give us what is running over? I believe that once we have had what we need, what is running over is meant for me to give to others. Remember that this verse starts with "give". It becomes a righteous cycle. The more I give, the more God pours into my lap. Consequently the more He pours into my lap, the more I am able to give. Being rich therefore is meant to make me a giver.

GOD'S GENEROSITY

God's generosity is seen in the story of Job. The first verse of the first chapter of the Book of Job opens up with an introduction to a blameless and upright man, who feared God and shunned evil. In many people's minds, a man of this description must be of a very humble demeanor. He probably just has enough to feed his family, and does not seek to be rich. In our contemporary church, he would probably be the pastor, an elder, a deacon or head of the youth ministry. Very few people would equate being blameless and upright with being extremely rich! In the country where I come from, a lot of people equate being extremely rich with theft. It is believed in many quarters that those who are extremely rich have probably stolen the money from some unsuspecting citizens! Not so in the Book of Job. Verse 3 of chapter one goes on to tell us what this blameless and upright man owned. Job 1: 3 *"And he owned seven thousand sheep, three thousand camels, five hundred yoke of oxen and five hundred donkeys, and had a large number of servants."* The Bible tells us that this man was the greatest man among all the people of the East. Let me remind you that if Job lived in my country, he would have been considered a thief, fraudster and a person whose heart was far from God! There would be a lot of speculation concerning where he got this wealth from. He obviously would have been seen as a man who had stolen from the poor to enrich himself! The Book of Job is not silent concerning from where Job got this extravagant wealth. The person who actually blows Job's cover is Satan. In a conversation between God and Satan, God draws Satan's attention to Job's righteousness. Job 1:8 *"Then the Lord said to Satan, 'Have you considered my servant Job? There is no one on earth like him; he is blameless and upright, a man who fears God and shuns evil."*

The fact that Job is extremely rich does not seem to bother God at all. In fact He does not even refer to it. This is because Job had not let his immense wealth interfere with his relationship with God. Satan however draws God's attention to Job's wealth and tries to connect his relationship with God to the fact that God had greatly enriched him. Job 1:9-10 *"Does Job fear God for nothing?" Satan replied. "Have you not put a hedge around him and his household and everything he has? You have blessed the work of his hands, so that his flocks and herds are spread throughout the land."* Satan reveals to us that it was God who had given Job all the wealth that he had. God not only made Job the richest man among all the people in the East, He also put a hedge of protection around that wealth so that he would not lose it! We see in the story of Job how generous and extravagant God can be towards a person who is blameless, upright, who fears Him, and hates evil. Job's story drives a wedge through the theory that God does not want His children to be rich.

ABRAHAM

In the story of Abraham, we also see the generosity of God. God had asked Abraham to leave his country and go to a place He would show him. Abraham obeyed God and left his homeland Haran with his wife and family, at the age of seventy- five. Lot, his nephew, also came with him. The Bible does not tell us how wealthy Abraham was when he left Haran, but in Genesis 13:2 we are told, *"Abram had become very wealthy in livestock and in silver and gold."*

Abraham is not the only one who acquired wealth. It seems like Lot also benefitted from his association with his uncle. Genesis 13:5-6 *" Now Lot, who was moving about with Abram, also had flocks and herds and tents. But the land could not support them while they stayed together, for their possessions were so great that they were not able to stay together."* The wonderful news is that by association with Abraham, we too can share in his blessing and one of the ways God blessed him was by making him very wealthy. Galatians 3:13 say that Jesus Christ redeemed us from the curse of the law through His death on the cross. However the exciting part of this redemption is seen in Galatians 3:14,16,29 *"He redeemed us in order that the blessing given to Abraham might come to the Gentiles through Christ Jesus...The promises were spoken to Abraham and to his seed...If you belong to Christ, then you are Abraham's seed, and heirs according to the promise."*

It is wonderful to know that God's generosity did not end with Abraham, but has also extended to us who believe in the Lord Jesus Christ! Abraham's seed should never be found lounging in poverty, lack and struggling! We are heirs to a promise of wealth and prosperity.

GOD'S PROVISION

Any caring and able parent would want to make provision for the needs of his or her children. Our loving Father has made provision for us to have what we need. In Deuteronomy 8:18 God told the Israelites, *"But remember the Lord your God, for it is He who gives you the ability to produce wealth, and so confirms the covenant, which He swore to your fathers, as it is today."* God wants us to remember that it is He who gives us the ability to produce wealth. So it is quite in order when we pray, to thank God for this ability and to ask that divine ideas on how to produce wealth will be downloaded from the heavenly Throne room! This kind of prayer is wonderful when a person is thinking of starting a business. Good business ideas are from God and this knowledge is available to every child of God. The second part of the verse tells us that when God gives His children the ability to make wealth, He is confirming the covenant that He made with our fathers. What covenant did God make with our fathers? Whenever God refers to the fathers, He is always talking about Abraham, Isaac and Jacob. In Genesis 12:2 God made a solemn promise to Abraham. *"I will make you into a great nation and I will bless you; I will make your name great, and you will be a blessing."* God blesses us to be a blessing. Part of this covenant meant that Abraham would become very wealthy in livestock and in silver and in gold (Genesis 13:2). We have already seen that this promise was not for Abraham alone, but through Jesus Christ, this promise extends to you and me (Galatians 3:16,29).

We have a covenant with God for Him to give us the ability to make wealth! Why then are so many Christians languishing in poverty? It starts with a way of thinking, and this way of thinking is cultural rather than biblical - A Christian culture that views poverty as humility.

In 2 Corinthians 8:9 the Bible says, *"For you know the grace of our Lord Jesus Christ, that though He was rich, yet for your sakes he became poor, so that you through his poverty might become rich.*" There are people who think that they do not deserve to be rich. Grace means that you do not deserve it. There is no Christian who deserves to be rich. We do not become rich because we are fasting and praying. We become rich because Christ desired it for us, and it had nothing to do with our deeds! Christ became poor so that I might be rich before I was even born! I believe that those who receive this wonderful revelation will live the rich life that Jesus provided for through His poverty. We need to start by rejecting poverty. Jesus does not want us to be poor. Period. If you cannot move beyond this fact then prepare yourself for a life of poverty - Then Jesus became poor for nothing. Jesus did not suffer poverty for nothing. He became poor so that we might be rich. He made this wonderful provision for every child of God. All we need is faith to believe the truth in the Word of God. However if we do not know what the Word says then we will miss out on its blessing!

WE ARE ALREADY RICH

I am sure that there are people who are thinking, "How can you say we are already rich when I am as poor as a Church mouse?" 2 Peter 1:3 say that "*His divine power has given us everything we need for life and godliness through our knowledge of him who called us by his own goodness.*" The Word of God tells us that God has given us everything we need for life and godliness. Does this include my rent and school fees for my children? Yes it does! But how come I don't have the school fees and the rent?

All God's blessings are spiritual. They are in the realm of the spirit. Ephesians 1:3 say "*Praise be to the God and Father of our Lord Jesus Christ, who has blessed us in the heavenly realms with every spiritual blessing in Christ.*" We have to first see the blessings with our spiritual eyes before they manifest before our physical eyes. It is for this very reason that we are told to speak of things that are not as though they are. The Bible exhorts the poor to **say,** "I am rich." I am rich because the Word of God says so. I must believe by faith in the Word of God that I am already rich! Nothing will manifest in my life physically that I have not believed exists spiritually. The school fees for my child has already been provided for by God spiritually through the promise of His Word which say, "***His divine power has given us everything we need for life...***" How do we bring things from the spiritual realm to manifest in the physical realm? Surely I cannot go to my child's school and tell the headmaster that I have brought with me invisible spiritual money. He will think I am crazy! Bringing spiritual things into the physical realm requires **saying or speaking in faith.** I believe by faith that I already have it according to the Word of God, then I **say** that I already have it! As long as the Word of God promises it, it is already mine. "***All God's promises are yes and amen in Christ Jesus.***" Once I have believed in my heart what the Word of God has provided, and have declared with my mouth that I already have it then I can wait in hope, certain that it will manifest in God's due time. Thereafter I can have peace that passes all understanding as I keep my mind, on Christ Jesus!

We must believe that God is a good and generous God whose greatest joy is to see us prosper. Believing anything less than this becomes a barrier to experiencing the provision of God. Our mindset is an important key that opens the door to our blessings.

PRAYER

Heavenly Father, I bring repentance for not seeing Your heart as it truly is. Because of the financial problems that I have gone through, I have believed that You intentionally let us go through financial problems so that we can grow from the suffering. I thank You for being a kind Father. I choose to believe that You have made provision for me to be rich. I thank You for Your generosity. I thank You for letting me see Your heart of love and kindness towards me. Thank You Lord for giving me all that I need. Teach me how to manifest on earth, the things that You have already provided for me in the spiritual realm. I come against the mind-controlling spirits that misrepresented You. I command every mind-controlling spirit to leave me now in the name of Jesus Christ! **Doubt, Confusion and fear**, come out in Jesus name! Breathe out through your mouth until you feel relief. You might yawn or cough or feel sensations in you hands and feet. He who the Son sets free is free indeed! – Amen!

CHAPTER 2

GOD'S PURPOSE FOR WEALTH

Alexander The Great was one of the greatest military leaders of all time. He was King of Macedonia and conqueror of the Persian Empire. It is said that before he died he left three instructions:

1) The best doctors in the world should carry his coffin.
2) The wealth he had accumulated (Money, Gold, Precious Stones) should be scattered along the procession to the cemetery.
3) His hands should be let loose, so they hang outside the coffin for all to see.

The three lessons that Alexander wanted to teach the world are that firstly, in the face of death the best doctors in the world cannot heal you. Secondly, was that material wealth acquired on earth will remain on earth. Thirdly, and the final point, is that we come into the world empty-handed and we will leave empty-handed!

If I am not going to my grave with gold and silver, then what is the purpose for wealth? Why be wealthy, if I do not have the ability to take it with me when I die? Why would Jesus be poor so that we might be rich? No one can argue with the fact that wealth is temporary. None of us is going to take any of our wealth with us when we die. Job 1:20

warn us, *"Naked I came from my mother's womb, and naked I will depart."* Looking at our world today, it is obvious that the better part of our waking hours, are spent working to make wealth. Stories of family members killing each other to acquire property left behind by a deceased rich relative are quite rampant in the country where I live.

Psalm 49:16-19 are very sobering verses that should stop any person pursuing the dream to be very rich in their tracks. *"Do not be envious when a man grows rich, when the splendor of his house increases, for he will take nothing with him when he dies, his splendor will not descend with him. Though while he lived he counted himself blessed – and men will praise you when you prosper – he will join the generation of his fathers, who will never see the light of day."*

This is a paradox that needs to be answered. Surely God must have a good reason for giving His children the ability to make wealth. If being rich is evil, as some people believe then why would God send His Son to be poor so that we may be rich?

Exodus chapter 12 recounts to us the climax and effect of the ten plagues that God sent on the Egyptians before they finally accepted to let the children of Israel leave their land. The last plague that God sent was the death of every first -born in the whole land! This was the message that Moses gave to Pharaoh before he left his presence for the last time. Exodus 11:4-6 *""...This is what the Lord says: 'About midnight I will go throughout Egypt. Every firstborn son in Egypt will die, from the firstborn son of Pharaoh, who sits on the throne, to the firstborn son of the slave girl, who is at her hand mill, and all the firstborn cattle as well..."*

What an unimaginable tragedy! This was truly going to be the darkest night in Egypt's history. The Bible records that Pharaoh and all his officials and all the Egyptians got up at midnight, and there was loud wailing in Egypt, for there was not a house without someone dead! This was the final plague that caused Pharaoh to finally let the Israelites leave his country. The Egyptians urged the Israelites to hurry and leave. I can only imagine the commotion in Egypt as the Israelites hurriedly pack their belongings in the dead of night! Then God gave Moses a very confusing instruction. He told Moses to ask the Egyptians for articles of silver and gold and for clothing. Exodus 12:36 says, *"The Lord had made the Egyptians favorably disposed toward the people, and they gave them what they asked for; so they plundered the Egyptians."*

Why would God ask the Israelites to ask the Egyptians for wealth? What did they need it for? After all they were going to wander about in the wilderness for 40 years! How was, the silver, gold and clothing going to benefit them in the desert? It was not just a little wealth. King David in the Book of Psalm tells us, *"He brought out Israel laden with silver and gold..."* - Psalm 105:37. There was nothing to buy in the desert neither did they need the clothes that the Egyptians gave them, in the hot wilderness. God always has a good purpose for everything that He does and in Exodus 35, we finally see the reason why God instructed the Israelites to ask the Egyptians for silver, gold and clothing.

When Moses went back to Mount Sinai to get the second set of Stone Tablets with the Ten Commandments written on them, God asked him to go back to the camp and make a Tabernacle where he would put the Ark of The Covenant. Moses asked the people to make an offering to the Lord for the building of the Tabernacle. Exodus 35:4-6 *"Moses said to the whole Israelite community, 'This is what the Lord has commanded: From what you have, take an offering for the Lord. Everyone who is willing is to bring to the Lord an offering of gold, silver and bronze; blue, purple and scarlet yarn and fine linen..."* Several things stand out from this verse.

1)   From what you have, take an offering for the Lord.
2)   Everyone who is willing is to bring to the Lord an offering.
3)   The offering is what God instructed them to ask the Egyptians for.

Let us look at these points one by one. Firstly, God never asks us for what we do not have. God knew that the Israelites had the offering He was asking for. Secondly, nobody was forced to give an offering to God. They could choose to keep what they had. Only those who were willing were to bring an offering to the Lord. It had to be a freewill offering. Unfortunately in many churches, the congregants are coerced or forced to give offerings with threats of the devourer coming to steal their wealth if they do not give. Sometimes those who do not give are shamed publicly. There is a denomination in my country where if you do not give tithes and offering then the clergy threaten to not conduct your funeral! The third point, points us to why God asked them to ask the Egyptians for silver, gold and clothing. He was going to need these items for the building of the Tabernacle.

How did the Israelites respond to this request from Moses? Exodus 35:21 *"And everyone who was willing and whose heart moved him came and brought an offering to the Lord for the work on the Tent of Meeting, for all its service, and for the sacred garments."* The Word of God tells us that He is the same yesterday, today and forever. What God required of the Israelites, He also requires of us today. 2 Corinthians 9:7 *"Each man should give what he has decided in his heart to give, not reluctantly or under compulsion, for God loves a cheerful giver."* God gave the Israelites the opportunity to give as they had made up their minds, with a willing heart! We see therefore that the Word of God is clearly against requiring people to give against their will. Because the Israelites felt no compulsion or manipulation for them to give, they gave cheerfully. Exodus 35:29 *"All the Israelite men and women who were willing brought to the Lord freewill offerings for all the work the Lord through Moses had commanded them to do."* They understood that it was God who had given them that wealth to begin with, so they gave out of a grateful heart. If we understood that when God asks us to give, we are only giving back to Him what He has given to us, perhaps we would be more willing to give cheerfully and willingly to His projects!

God earmarked Bezalel and Oholiab, whom He gave supernatural skill and ability to oversee the work of building the Tabernacle. We are told, *"...And every skilled person to whom the Lord had given ability and who was willing to come and do the work,"* was summoned by Moses to help Bezalel and Oholiab. These skilled workmen received from Moses the offering the Israelites had brought to carry out the work of constructing the sanctuary. Then the workers encountered a problem that caused them to stop working. Exodus 26:3 *"... And the people continued to bring freewill offerings morning after morning. So all the skilled craftsmen who were doing all the work on the sanctuary left their work."* How could this be a problem? What was wrong with the people bringing offerings morning after morning? The workmen went to Moses with a complaint. What was the complaint? *"...The people are bringing more than enough for doing the work the Lord commanded to be done."* – Exodus 36:5. The people are bringing more than enough! That was the problem? How many churches today have ever encountered such a problem? Often Pastors have to beg their congregants to give money towards church projects! From this passage of Scripture it is obvious that people give more when they are given the opportunity to give willingly as they have made up their minds. These Israelites kept bringing their freewill offerings morning by morning. They just gave and gave until it became a problem. How did Moses handle this problem? *"Then Moses gave an order and they sent this word throughout the camp: 'No man or woman is to make anything else for the sanctuary."* Can you imagine a situation where a church has a project and people give so much that it becomes a problem and the pastor has to tell people not to give anymore? There are two remarkable things that we can note from this verse. The first thing is the people's willingness to give and the second thing is the honesty of the workmen. Unfortunately many churches would be just too willing to continue receiving offerings even after the target has been met. After Moses sent out this command, the people would not be denied the joy of giving. They ignored Moses and continued to bring more offerings! *"And so the people were restrained from bringing more, because what they already had was more then enough to do the work."* Wouldn't it be wonderful to have this kind of problem in our churches and ministries, where people have to be restrained from giving because they have already given more than enough? So why does God give His children wealth? God gives us wealth because He has projects for His kingdom that require money. He gives us so that we can also give, and tells us, *"...It is more blessed to give than to receive."* – Acts 20:35. We have seen in chapter one that God has a generous heart towards His children and that He wants His children to be rich. Below are some of God's commands to the rich.

1 Timothy 6:17-18

> *"Command those who are rich in this present world not to be arrogant nor put their hope in wealth, which is so uncertain, but to put their hope in God, who richly provides us with everything for our enjoyment. Command them to do good, to be rich in good deeds, and to be generous and willing to share."*

1 John 3:17

> *"If anyone has material possessions and sees his brother in need but has no pity on him, how can the love of God be in him?"*

Proverbs 22:9

> *"A generous man will himself be blessed for he shares his food with the poor"*

Proverbs 28:27

> *"He who gives to the poor will lack nothing, but he who closes his eyes to them receives many curses."*

PRAYER

Heavenly Father, I thank you for the example of how generous and willing to give, the Israelites were. They understood that whatever they had, had come from you. You give to us so that we can also give. Please forgive me for not being a cheerful giver. Change my heart dear Father. Everything I have has come from you. Forgive me for acting as though it is through my own strength that I have made my wealth. You have kept me well so that I am able to work. It is You who has given me the wisdom and ability to make wealth. Thank you for providing everything for my enjoyment. Please help me be aware of the needs of the people that You bring around me. I commit myself by Your grace, to be rich in good deeds, and to be generous and willing to share. You do not ask me to give what I don't have. Help me realize that it is more blessed to give than to receive. I commit to willingly give for Your projects. I come against the spirits of **selfishness, greed and covetousness**. I command them to leave me now in the name of Jesus Christ! Breathe out through your mouth until you feel relief. You might yawn or cough or feel sensations in you hands and feet. He who the Son sets free is free indeed! – Amen!

CHAPTER
3

FINANCIAL PRINCIPLES FOR NEW BELIEVERS

L ife has divided the stages of growth for the human being into many categories – Infants, Babies, Toddlers, Pre-teens, Teenagers, Youth, Adults, Middle age, and Elderly. Yet in the Christian life it is often assumed that once we become born again, everybody is on the same level. God calls Himself our Father, and we, His children. The title of "A child of God" then, is used for every Believer whether a Christian for one day or for fifty years. It is therefore important when we are reading the Bible, to know which group of Believers God is addressing. The way one talks to an infant is not the way that one talks to an elderly person. What separates the infant from the adult person? It is growth and experience that has led to maturity. Therefore, the commands that are in the Bible for infant Christians are different from the commands that are in the Bible for the mature adult Christian, and it is important to know the difference.

1 Peter 2: 2-3 tells us, *"Like newborn babies, crave pure spiritual milk, so that by it you may grow up in your salvation, now that you have tasted that the Lord is good."* A New-born Believer is exhorted to treat the Word of God the same way that a new-born treats milk. One just needs to go to a nursery in a hospital to hear

how the infants scream to be fed. Babies need milk so that they can grow. An infant that is fed milk consistently but does not grow has a serious problem. In a similar way a new-born Believer that is fed the Word of God consistently but does not grow has a serious problem. There is nothing wrong with being an infant, but there is something wrong with not growing! A twenty-five year old that is still wearing diapers has a serious problem whereas a mother is very happy to put a diaper on her infant.

Hebrews 5:13 give us a principle that is worth noting. *"Anyone who lives on milk, being still an infant, is not acquainted with the teaching about righteousness."* If the infant Believer is not acquainted with the teaching about righteousness then there are certain things that God will not require of an infant Believer, until they mature. So what does the Bible tell this group of Believers about wealth and finances?

Matthew 7:7 *"Ask and it will be given to you; seek and you will find; knock and the door will be opened to you."* Infant Believers are encouraged to ask and they will be given. To seek and they will find. To knock and the door will be opened to them. In fact when I first became a Believer, God seemed to give me everything I asked for. For a young Believer, asking and receiving is what builds faith in God. They see God as a provider and learn to depend on God and not on the things that they had put their hopes on prior to joining the household of faith.

Many times we forget that Jesus' disciples were infants. They had only been Believers for three and a half years by the time Jesus left them. In John 16:23-24 we see Jesus speaking to His disciples just before He goes back to heaven. *"…I tell you the truth, my Father will give you whatever you ask in my name…Ask and you will receive, and your joy will be full."* What do infants, toddlers and young children ask for? - Milk, Sweets, and Toys etc. Most parents who are able will gladly give their child these things. Once they receive these things from their parents, their joy is full. I am always amazed at how easy it is to please a small child. However if their thirty- year-old child keeps asking for things, there will be understandable tension in the relationship! There is an expectation that as children grow older, they will become less and less dependent on receiving things from their parents and start to create their own wealth. 1 Corinthians 13:10-12 gives a very vivid picture of this expectation.

"But when perfection comes, the imperfect disappears. When I was a child, I talked like a child, I thought like a child, I reasoned like a child. When I became a man, I put childish ways behind me...now I see but a poor reflection as in a mirror...Now I know in part...Then I shall know fully."

Children are at the center of their world! Everything is about them. Most children are selfish and want the best for themselves. Most children hate to share and believe that their parents' job is to give them whatever they want. It is a common sight to see a child screaming is a supermarket, because their parent has said that they cannot get a particular toy! Many young Believers act like this with God. They see themselves as depleted and needing many things from God. I will reiterate that there is nothing wrong with being an infant and there is nothing wrong with asking God for things. He, Himself, encourages us to ask Him for things as our heavenly Father. Matthew 7:11 says, *"If you, then, though you are evil, know how to give good gifts to your children, how much more will your Father in heaven give good gifts to those who ask him!"*

Are you are young Believer? Ask God for your needs. He is your Father and loves you and will provide all your needs. Asking and receiving requires faith. Believe that God is faithful to provide what He has promised in His Word. Wait in hope and trust knowing that God's Word can never fail and He has promised that if you ask, you will receive. Do not be discouraged when you have to wait for the answers. God is growing your faith. To you Jesus says in John 15:7, *"If you remain in me and my words remain in you, ask whatever you wish, and it will be given to you."*

PRAYER FOR YOUNG BELIEVERS

Heavenly Father, thank you for Your Word that I can stand on. You have told me to ask and I will receive. I thank you that You are always faithful to your promises. Before I came to You I believed that I had to work hard and depend on my own strength to get what I need. I believed the false saying, "God helps those who help themselves." You help me because I cannot help myself. Teach me to depend on You in total trust. You are my provider. Your Word says, *"And my God will meet all your needs according to his glorious riches in Christ Jesus."* Help me believe Your Word by the power of the Holy Spirit. I know that You know all my needs and as I ask you for them, You will answer. You are a good and compassionate God. Thank you for loving me. I now come against the spirit of **self-reliance, doubt, fear of asking, insecurity, self-pity, self-doubt and greed** in the name of Jesus! Come out of me right now! You have no place in my life. Breathe out through your mouth until you feel relief. You might yawn or cough or feel sensations in you hands and feet. He who the Son sets free is free indeed! I pray all this with thanksgiving in the name of Jesus Christ – Amen!

FINANCIAL PRINCIPLES FOR
MATURE BELIEVERS

A time comes when God expects the young Believer to grow to the next level. This is a principle that we see at play across all aspects of life. Growth is what confirms that an organism is alive and healthy. The Christian life is no different. When we move to the next stage of maturity, God expects us to stop talking like a child, thinking like a child and reasoning like a child. Every child of God must strive towards perfection and we are going to see in this chapter, what perfection looks like when it comes to our financial needs. In 1 Corinthians 13:10, the child is called "imperfect." Imperfect in the way they talk, think and reason. We are going to see that the Bible addresses mature Believers in a very different way from the way it addresses young Believers. If we do not see the difference then we will conclude that the Bible contradicts itself, which is very far from the truth!

Paul, in writing to the Hebrew Church, lamented that he had much to say to them, but he could not because they had not matured as he had expected. Hebrews 5:11 *"We have much to say about this, but it is hard to explain because you are slow to learn."* Paul was disappointed that though this church should have matured to the point that he could speak to them as mature Believers, in their talking, thinking and reasoning, they were still in the infant stage. *"In fact, though by this time you ought to be teachers, you need someone to teach you the elementary truths of God's word all over again. You need milk, not solid food."*

What is solid food when it comes to finances? It is eventually coming to the realization that as a mature Believer, we do not have to ask God for anything! 2 Peter 1:3 is talking to mature Believers and tells them, *"His divine power has given us everything we need for life and godliness through our knowledge of him who called us by his own glory and goodness."*

While the baby Christian asks for things, the mature Believer receives by faith, what he or she believes has already been provided for through the death of Jesus Christ on the Cross of Calvary. How do I believe that when I still have needs? When I am still struggling financially and cannot pay my bills? We need to understand that there is nothing that Jesus is providing for anyone today. Everything that Jesus ever needed to provide, He provided for us when He died on the Cross of Calvary. When Jesus said, "It is finished," what, did He mean? It meant that He had provided forever all that mankind would ever need in life. He provided a blessing, instead of the curse that was upon mankind (Galatians 3:13). He provided righteousness, instead of the sin that mankind was wallowing in (2 Corinthians 5:21). He provided health for the sick (1 Peter 2:24), and HE PROVIDED RICHES FOR THE POOR (2 Corinthians 8:9). Whatever we say must be in line with the truth of God's Word and that is why Joel 3:10 says, *"Let the weak say I am strong."* If the weak can say "I am strong!" then the poor can also say *"I am rich!"* We must believe by faith that God has already provided the things that we believe Him for. Where are these things? They are in the heavenly and spiritual realms. Ephesians 1:3 *"Praise be to the God and Father of our Lord Jesus Christ who has blessed us in the heavenly realms with every spiritual blessing in Christ."* The verse does not say that God will bless us, but who has already blessed us. So how I approach God is very important when I need something to manifest for me in the physical realm. For example if I need money for rent, how do I approach God? I approach Him as a heavenly Father who has already provided my rent in the spiritual realms. However rent in the spiritual realms, will not be accepted by my landlord. He needs to see his money in the physical realm! It is therefore very important to know how to get my rent to manifest in the natural and physical realm.

In Mark 11:24 we see a principle worth noting when it comes to getting things to manifest from the spiritual realm to the physical realm. *"Therefore I tell you, whatever you ask for in prayer, believe that you have received it and it will be yours."* Really? All I need to do is believe that I have received it and it will be mine? The answer is yes, if you can believe it! The challenge is in my believing that I have already received something that I cannot see with my physical eyes. Lack of faith is the biggest hindrance to receiving things from God. As we read in Hebrews 11:1, *"Now faith is being sure of what we hope for and certain of what we do not see."* Faith is backed up by belief in the faithfulness of God. If God has said it then it is true and I can believe it. The more I totally believe in the fact that God is faithful to keep His promise, the more things will manifest in my life. Let us take for example the issue of the rent that I need, to pay my landlord. What is the first thing that I need to do? I need to find a verse where God has promised to provide my needs. Let us take Philippians 4:19 *"And my God will meet all your needs according to his glorious riches in Christ Jesus."* We need to understand that God is only duty bound to do what He has promised to do in His Word. The Bible tells us that God watches over His Word to perform it (Jeremiah 1:12). Isaiah 55:11, also exhorts us to believe what God has promised us in His Word. *"So is my word that goes out from my mouth: It will not return to me empty, but will accomplish what I desire and achieve the purpose for which I sent it."* The Word of God is activated to produce what it promises in the physical realm when I believe it and act upon it. Faith without works is dead (James 2:17), and dead faith will not manifest anything. So how do I make my faith active? Once I identify the verse with the promise that God has made concerning what I am asking for, then I declare it verbally. "Father You have said in Your Word that it is You who supplies all my needs. You have also said in Your Word that Your divine power has given me everything I need for life and godliness. I believe that You have already provided my rent." This is a declaration that is made by faith believing in a God who does not lie. *"God is not a man that He should lie, nor a son of man that he should change his mind. Does he speak and then not act? Does he promise and not fulfill?"* – Numbers 23:19. What is the final act in this chain of events that leads to actually holding what I need in my hands? I say "Thank You Lord for providing my rent". Whenever somebody gives us something, the polite thing to say is "Thank you." Once I have acknowledged that I have already received the rent, I move on and do not ask God for my rent again. This is where "The peace that passes all understanding," comes in. It passes understanding because, how can I have peace when I do not have the rent in my hands? I think that we can now understand why the Bible tells us to fight the good fight of faith (1 Timothy 6:12). Faith is a fight because my senses will oppose me fiercely! – What I feel, see, and hear. I may start to feel fearful that it is almost the end of the month yet I still do not have the rent in my hands. I may see a threatening letter from the landlord. What should I do? I should focus on the promise that God has given me in His Word and the fact that He is faithful, while continuing to thank God that He has already provided! This is the good fight of faith!

Another enemy that I have to fight is my mouth. Many people do not seem to be aware, that our life, is driven by our mouth!

The Bible tells us that in the tongue, is the power of life and death (Proverbs 18:21). We are made in the image of God and so we operate as God operates. In the Book of Genesis, God created everything through His Word. In the same way, our words have power to create whatever we say. What have you been saying about your financial situation? Unfortunately there are people who are always talking about their lack. "I am so broke this month, I do not know how I will pay my rent!" By saying this, you have created a situation of lack to the point that you cannot pay your rent. Remember that the weak say that they are strong and the poor say that they are rich. These are not just idle words that we say for the sake of saying them. When I say, "I am well provided for by my heavenly Father", it should come from a position of faith and trust in the promises of God. Satan listens to what we say. As soon as we say that we are poor, he will accuse us before God. "She does not believe that you have already provided. She is speaking contrary to Your word, therefore I have the right to block her rent!" Revelation 12:10 tell us that Satan, the Accuser of the brethren, accuses us before God day and night! He accuses us of saying things that are contrary to the Word of God. Let us use our mouths to create the financial situation that we want. The Bible tells us that we speak out of the abundance of our hearts. If my heart is full of faith then I will speak faith. Faith comes by hearing the Word of God. Let us therefore fill our hearts with faith from the Word of God!

To get a harvest, we must sow a seed. What is the seed that we sow? It is the Word of God. Mark 4:14 *"The farmer sows the word."* Every word that we speak is a seed being sown and you can be sure that you will reap a harvest from it. So if I need a financial harvest, I need to go to the bag of seeds (The Bible) and get a seed that corresponds to the kind of harvest that I need. Once I find the seed then I sow it in my heart, a miracle happens! Mark 4:27 *"Night and day, whether he sleeps or gets up, the seed sprouts and grows, though he does*

*not know how. All by itself the soil produces grain – first the stalk,
then the head, then the full kernel in the head. As soon as the grain
is ripe, he puts the sickle to it, because the harvest has come."* The
Bible promises us that when we sow the Word of God, it eventually
produces a harvest! A mature believer hears the Word, accepts it, and
sows it in his or her heart. How do we sow the Word in our hearts?
By believing it, declaring it by faith then giving thanks! Giving
thanks is what proves that I believe I have already received. While
asking places the responsibility for receiving on God, receiving by
faith places the responsibility on me. What is God's part after I have
sowed the seed? He waters it (Isaiah 55:10).

A mature believer understands grace. Grace means, undeserved
favor. We receive by faith, what grace has already provided. That
means that I do not work for what I receive from God. Baby
Christians believe that they can make God give them what they want
by fasting and doing religious duties. Mature believers know that no
amount of fasting will release what Christ did not already provide
through His death on the cross of Calvary! We cannot twist God's
arm to give us anything through fasting. Fasting simply crucifies the
flesh and quiets it so that we can hear the voice of God more clearly.

Have you been asking for things that you used to ask for before
and received, yet now you ask and do not receive? You have matured
and God wants you to move to the next level of receiving by faith.

PRAYER FOR MATURE BELIEVERS

Heavenly Father, I thank you for all that I have learned by reading
this chapter. I now realize that since I have been a Christian for
over ten years, You expect spiritual growth from me. Forgive me for
not reading Your Word often enough for me to grow in my faith.
Forgive me for talking, thinking and reasoning like a child! I have

kept asking and asking instead of believing that You have already provided. Please help me understand that You have already provided everything that I need in this life. Help me see the things that You have already provided, with the eyes of faith. I cancel all the negative words that I have spoken concerning my finances, in the name of Jesus Christ! Now I command all spirits of **mind control, negativity, lack of faith, fear, insecurity, doubt, manipulation, impatience, worry, anxiety, restlessness, frustration, greed, covetousness and material lus**t to leave me now in the name of Jesus Christ! You have no place in my life! Come out of me right now in the powerful name of Jesus Christ! Breathe out through your mouth until you feel relief. You might yawn or cough or feel sensations in you hands and feet. He who the Son sets free is free indeed! Thank You Jesus for setting me free! – Amen!

CHAPTER
5

EATING OUR SEED

There are valuable lessons that we can learn from farmers. You cannot be a farmer if you do not have seeds to sow. Where do seeds come from? Seeds come from the harvest, and you cannot have a harvest if you do not start with seeds. A similar analogy is that chickens come from eggs and eggs come from chickens. One cannot exist without the other. It is therefore very important for a farmer to have seed for sowing, if he expects to get a harvest. Therefore when a farmer harvests, he cannot consume all the harvest. He must put aside some seed to sow back into the ground. Growing up as a child, I did not understand why after harvesting maize, my mother would not allow us to eat everything but would put aside some seed, which she called in our local language, "kodhi". The kodhi would be spread outside in the sun on plastic gunny bags until the maize seeds were very dry. After that she would gather these dry seeds and put them in our granary. It is interesting to note that the maize that she would boil or roast for us to eat was called "Oduma". We never ever ate the kodhi. The same principal works in the spiritual realm. In Isaiah 55:10, God tells us that He sends rain and snow to the earth to make seeds bud and flourish. What does this process yield? *"...So that it yields seed for the sower and bread for the eater."* What God calls here "Seed for the sower" is what my mother called "Kodhi" while the "Bread for the eater" is what my mother called "Oduma".

We can see how important it is to put back seed into the ground, if we hope to continue reaping a harvest. We cannot afford to eat our seed. It would have been very unwise for my mother to treat all the harvest as Oduma to feed her children. No matter how much we longed for it, my wise mother never let us eat the Kodhi. A harvest is totally dependent on seed. It is however imperative that we differentiate the seed from the bread. I should not eat the seed or sow the bread. The bread is what is supposed to sustain me while I wait for the next harvest. There are people who believe that it is ok to give God the whole harvest. In a way they feel that they are showing God how they have put their total trust in Him as the Provider. God IS the Provider. He provides seed for sowing and bread for eating. Bread is what God provides to put a roof over our heads, clothes on our backs and food on the table. A person who denies their children these necessities and instead gives it to the church is not obeying the Word of God which says in 1 Timothy 5:8 *"If anyone does not provide for his relatives, and especially for his immediate family, he has denied the faith and is worse than an unbeliever."* I have heard of individuals in my country who have sold household furniture so that they can give the money to a pastor who has told them that God will give them "A good measure, pressed down, shaken together and running over". These people have taken what rightfully belonged to their children in order to enrich a greedy "pastor". The Bible calls this giver, worse than an unbeliever. They have sown the children's bread!

I think that it is important to note that it is God Himself who provides the seed for sowing. 2 Corinthians 9:10 says, *"Now he who supplies seed to the sower and bread for food will also supply and increase the store of seed and will enlarge the harvest of your righteousness."* God is calling the sowing of seed, righteousness. Notice that what God is increasing is not the bread but the store of seed! This is because the sowing of more seed enlarges the harvest.

When we sow, we are simply giving back to God what He has provided. This means that no one can come to God and say that they have no seed to sow. My prayer therefore should be that God provides for me seed for sowing, so that the sowing can yield bread for eating. For a long time my prayer was for bread for eating! Once we understand this principle, we will not only sow bountifully, but cheerfully. Sowing does not do God a favor. Sowing does us a favor! 2 Corinthians 9:6 says *"Remember this: Whoever sows sparingly will also reap sparingly, and whoever sows generously will also reap generously."* Do you want a generous harvest? Then you need to sow more seed into your field. So we can see that whether my harvest is big or small does not depend on God but on me!

Once God has done His part, it is up to me what I do with the seed and the bread. Unfortunately many people eat their seed together with the bread. That is not wise. But how do we know what is the seed and what is the bread? Does God yield the seed and bread already marked for us? The answer is no. God gives us a harvest and within this harvest the seed and bread are mixed together. Let us say that God gives me 100,000 Kenya shillings. God does not tell me how much to give as an offering and how much to use on myself. 2 Corinthians 9:7 says, *"Each man should give what he has decided in his heart to give, not reluctantly or under compulsion, for God loves a cheerful giver."* Once my harvest comes, it should be up to me how much I want to sow back into the work of God. No Pastor or ministry leader should ever tell me how much I should give. God leaves that decision entirely up to me! What if I decide to give 10,000 Kenya shillings for the work of God, out of my 100,000 Kenya shillings harvest? You have done well to sow back seed into the ground, however when the harvest comes, do not expect a large harvest. Remember that the Word of God says that if you sow generously, you will also reap generously. Is giving 10% of your harvest generous? I think that we can all agree that giving 10% of your harvest is not generous. Why then do people sow 10% and expect a large harvest? Such people, neither know what the Word of God says, or understand it. Galatians 6:7 says *"... A man reaps what he sows."*

Many Christians often quote Luke 6:38 *"Give and it will be give to you. A good measure, pressed down, shaken together and running over, will be poured into your lap..."* This verse is often used as though any time you give, regardless of the amount, you should expect a big harvest. Many people ignore the last part of the verse, which says, *"For with the measure you use, it will be measured to you."*

In the parable of the sower, we are told that the only seed that produced a crop was the seed that was sown in good soil (Mark 4:20). However, note that the seed produced, thirty, sixty or a hundred fold what was sown. Why did it produce three different amounts? It is because some people sowed sparingly and got thirty fold. Others sowed a bit more generously and got sixty fold. However, some who understood the principle of how to get a bumper harvest sowed generously and reaped a hundred fold! How much you reap does not depend on God but on you! When we see a lot of increase in our lives, it is God giving us an opportunity to sow more, for a larger harvest.

When I was young and in Sunday school my father would give me "Sadaka." This little coin I was instructed, was to be put in the offering basket. All around me when I started to attend the main service, I would hear coins dropping into the offering basket during the offering time. I grew up knowing that God was given coins! I hardly saw anyone give money in the form of a note. As I grew up, and since I did no read the Bible for myself, I believed that giving offering was a duty to God. Also that we gave to Him anything small that we could afford. Needless to say, I grew up with a lot of financial lack because I hardly sowed and when I did, I did it very sparingly! It is the duty of every parent to teach their children about the connection between giving and receiving. Children should be taught that when we give, we are actually sowing a seed, which will yield a harvest. Indeed it is more blessed to give than to receive.

PRAYER

Heavenly Father, thank You that You are my provider. You are faithful to yield for me seed for sowing and bread for eating. You have promised to provide all my needs according to Your riches in glory by Christ Jesus. Thank you for teaching me today that when you provide financially, you do not expect me to use everything on myself. Please forgive me for not being faithful to sow back the seed into Your work. When I have sown back into Your work, it has been very little, yet I expect you to provide for me generously. I want to be able to give generously. Please provide seed for me so that I may be able to do that. Help me be the kind of person that gives so that I can reap a hundred fold. Your Word has told me that I should provide for my relatives and especially my immediate family. Forgive me where I have not provided for them. Forgive me where I have eaten my seed. Holy Spirit my total dependence is on you. Lord Jesus, cleanse me with Your blood and Father please render me not guilty of all these sins that I have committed. I want to be a cheerful and generous giver. I now command all spirits of **deception, greed, fear, poverty, lack, struggling, covetousness, and selfishness** to leave me now in the name of Jesus Christ. Come out of my mind, emotions, and will. I am the temple of the Holy Spirit and you have no place in me! Breathe out deeply until you feel relief. You might yawn or cough or feel sensations in you hands and feet. He who the Son sets free is free indeed! I am set free in the name of Jesus.– Amen!

CHAPTER

6

IDOLATRY AS A BARRIER TO WEALTH

Try and imagine a river with lots of water flowing down a slope from a mountain and providing water for agriculture and cattle to the community that is living down the valley. The community is grateful to God who they see as having provided water for them in abundance! Then a cement company that produces blocks comes and opens their factory further up on the mountain slope. They build a dam to harvest the water from the river, so that they can use it to make their cement blocks. It does not take long before the community living further down the mountain slope has very little water trickling down to them. They no longer have enough water for irrigation and their harvests are greatly affected! Their animals also start to suffer from lack of water. They have no idea that a factory has built a dam further up the mountain slope that is affecting their supply of water. The rural community thinks that it is God who is no longer sending them enough rain for water. No matter how much they pray for God to give them water, the river remains dry! They do not know that there is a barrier in the form of a dam that is blocking the water from reaching them.

Unfortunately many Christians are living down the mountain slopes where there is no water. They pray for water and although God has provided more than enough water to meet the need for "agriculture and cattle", the water is not reaching them because there is a "dam" stopping the water further up the slope.

A barrier often stands between us and what we want, or where we want to go. Like the dam that blocked the water from reaching the community, a barrier can make us come to the wrong conclusion. A barrier may cause us not to see the total picture. Worshiping other gods creates a barrier that blocks God's blessings from reaching us. Turning to anyone or anything for wisdom, knowledge and wealth rather than to the God and Father of the Lord Jesus Christ is idolatry. Idolatry is worshiping another god. God hates idolatry and metes out punishment to people who turn to other gods for help. In Deuteronomy 18:10-11 see what God calls idolatry. *"Let no one be found among you who sacrifices his son or daughter in the fire, who practices divination or sorcery, interprets omens, engages in witchcraft, or casts spells, or who is a medium or spiritist or who consults the dead. ANYONE WHO DOES THESE THINGS IS DETESTABLE TO THE LORD..."* (Emphasis mine).

It is hard to imagine God blessing anyone who is detestable to Him. It is therefore understandable why God said in Deuteronomy 28:29, concerning those who followed other gods and served them, *"...You will be unsuccessful in everything you do; day after day you will be oppressed and robbed with no one to rescue you."* I have counseled a lot of people who have told me that their life was stagnant and that anything that they put their hand to do would succeed for a little while then come crashed down. This was not because they were lazy or ignorant of their work. It seemed like an invisible force was working against them! They have also told me that this pattern seemed to follow many members of their immediate and extended family.

Exodus 20:3-5 tells us that God is a jealous God, who will not look away while people turn to other gods. He says that because of this grave sin, the descendants of those who worship other gods will suffer the same punishment that they themselves suffer. Lamentations 5:7 says *"Our fathers have sinned and are no more, but we bear their punishment."* Deuteronomy chapter 28 gives us 54 verses on the punishment that come on idolaters, and we have seen that one of the punishments is poverty and lack! In the previous chapter we were exhorted to sow much seed for a bumper harvest but now we encounter another principle. Deuteronomy 28:38 says *"You will sow much seed in the field but you will harvest little, because locusts will devour it."* Idolatry interferes with the principles of God. Worshiping other gods will deplete our wealth. You may argue that you do not worship other gods and that you have been a believer since childhood, and that your parents are also believers. Why then should the curse of poverty touch you? We have seen that four generations of the idolatrous person will be affected. That means that if your great grandfather went to see witchdoctors, or was a witchdoctor himself, then his children, grandchildren and great grandchildren will all suffer poverty. It will be a very conspicuous pattern that is obvious even to people looking from the outside. The general story in this extended family will be that people are working very hard and are highly educated, but lack and struggle is their daily portion!

In many countries in Africa, before Christianity came, the footsteps of anybody that had a problem ended at the front door of the witchdoctor's hut. The local witchdoctor became the go -to person for health, wealth and family challenges. Unknown to them, they passed on financial curses three generations down! As I teach on breaking generational curses, I often ask everybody to stand up for a small exercise. I then ask anybody whose great grandparents were believers and did not worship other gods to sit down. In every case, no one has ever sat down. I have then moved on to the next generation down (grandparents), and asked the same questions. Again nobody has ever sat down Finally I have asked if there was anybody in the room whose parents became believers in Jesus Christ at the age of thirteen, meaning that they had never been involved in witchcraft, sorcery, necromancy etc. Out of about 10,000 maybe 100 people have sat down. I have often brought to our attention in Africa, that many of us have come into Christianity with the baggage of four generations! How then are we able to live in prosperity? Many people in my country who come to our offices for counseling have themselves been taken to see witchdoctors by their parents or relatives and the financial devastation in their lives is often quite evident! I believe that much of the poverty that we see in Third World countries is as a result of rampant idolatrous practices in the bloodline.

Since many Africans are very religious, it is not hard to get them to go and see a witchdoctor. There is a warning in Isaiah 8:19 that is worth taking very seriously. *"When men tell you to consult mediums and spiritists, who whisper and mutter, should not a people inquire of their God? Why consult the dead on behalf of the living?"* I have met many people who tell me that they had a problem and a friend advised them to go and see a "Man of God" or a "Woman of God" who would pray for them and God would answer their requests. They have gone to the "Man of God," only to find out that the person turned out to be a false prophet out to enrich themself. One particular person told me that the "Prophet" asked them to come back with a certain amount of money and a white chicken! The man used demonic powers to tell them details about their past. They were taken in by all the truth that this person knew about them and became captive to the demonic powers. By the time this person realized that they had been duped, they had parted with a considerable amount of money! After this experience, this person lost their job and became destitute, relying on hand- outs from their friends and relatives. Worshiping other gods will bring a financial curse on a person and three generations after them!

God warned Israel not to worship other gods but they did not listen. They still went ahead and worshiped the gods of the nations around them. Listen to what God told them through Prophet Isaiah. *"When you spread your hands out in prayer, I will hide my eyes from you; even if you offer many prayers, I will not listen..."* Many pray and declare victory but do not see any change to their financial situation. The result is always frustration, and doubt in God's ability. In Ezekiel 8:18 God says, *"...Although they shout in my ears, I will not listen to them."* I can only imagine how frustrating and demoralizing it would be for God not to give ear to my prayer requests. It is understandable why a Believer would say like Malachi in chapter 3 and verse 14, *"...It is futile to serve God. What did we gain by carrying out his requirements and going about like mourners before the Lord Almighty?"* How many Christians think this in their hearts after they have prayed for years for a "financial breakthrough" and their situation has only gotten worse?

Jesus became a curse for us as we read in Galatians 3:13. If Jesus became a curse for me, then why should I still wallow under a curse of poverty? We must appropriate what Jesus did on the cross for us. In the same way although Jesus became sin for us (2 Corinthians 5:21), we still must appropriate what He did on the cross for us through salvation. Everybody is not saved because Jesus died for the sins of the whole world. Each person must accept that they are a sinner; Believe that Jesus became their sin; Repent of their sin; Confess that their sins have been dealt with and that they have accepted Christ into their hearts. In the very same way, to break the financial curse we must accept that because of our idolatry we are under the curse. Secondly we must believe that Christ has become our curse. Thirdly we must repent. What do we repent about? Daniel gives us an example through his prayer when they were under the curse and slaves in Babylon. *"O Lord, in keeping with all your righteous acts, turn away your anger and your wrath from Jerusalem, your city, your holy hill. Our sins and the iniquities of our father have made Jerusalem and your people an object of scorn to all those around us."*

– Daniel 9:16. Daniel was a righteous man and yet his righteousness did not keep the curse from taking him as a slave to Babylon. Many people believe that if they live a righteous life, financial blessings will fall on them automatically. That is not so. When it comes to the curse of idolatry, EVERYBODY is touched. Listen to what God tells the prophet Ezekiel to tell Jerusalem who was under the curse in Babylon. Ezekiel 21:3-4 *"This is what the Lord says: I am against you. I will draw my sword from its scabbard and cut off from you the righteous and the wicked. Because I am going to cut off the righteous and the wicked, my sword will be unsheathed against EVERYONE from south to north."* – Emphasis mine. When it comes to the curse nobody is exempt. But praise God that we have a curse -breaker and His name is Jesus Christ!

PRAYER

Heavenly Father, thank you for teaching me how idolatry has affected me financially. I now understand that the idolatry of my forefathers has affected me. As I pray Father I ask that You will deliver me from every satanic bondage that my finances are under because of idolatry. Please remove every legal right that Satan has had to touch my finances. I confess the sins of my forefathers who worshiped other gods. I stand guilty before You. Lord Jesus, let Your blood cleanse all my sins. Father pass a verdict of "Not guilty!" over me. Set me free by the finished work of the Cross of Jesus Christ.

As a servant of the Living God I take authority and break every curse over my life! All my generations back to Adam! I renounce and denounce their shrines, altars, dedications, spoken curses, broken promises, vows, covenants, oaths, libations, traditions, blood sacrifices and incantations that connected me to evil and dark satanic forces! I declare that my finances are set free from the control and manipulation of evil spirits! I am set free right now in the name of Jesus Christ! He who the Son sets free is free indeed! I now take authority and command the evil spirits of **witchcraft, occult, divination, sorcery necromancy, astrology, water spirits, serpentine spirits, cult spirits, black, red, green and white magic, poverty, lack, struggling, broke, no money, no favor, no promotion and failure,** to leave me now in Jesus name! You must leave right now in the name of Jesus Christ! Be gone in Jesus name! Out! Blow out through your mouth until you feel relief. You might yawn or cough or feel sensations in you hands and feet. He who the Son sets free is free indeed! I am set free in Jesus name! – Amen!

CHAPTER 7

CURSE OF THE FLYING SCROLL

I learnt about the curse of the Flying Scroll after many years of frustration, distress and struggle! My husband and I have lived with our children in four different countries in Africa – Kenya, Zambia, Mauritania and Senegal (Total of twenty years).

In Kenya, Zambia and Mauritania our houses were broken into at night and our property stolen. While living in Senegal, the two front side- lights of our car was stolen in a very open place outside the church where one would not have expected that a person could steal. The guard told us that our car was the very first car to have been stolen from as far back as he could remember, and he had worked for the church for a long time!

While we lived in Kenya, our house was broken into two times. We were only two Christian families living in the gated community and each time our house was broken into, our neighbors heard about it and came to sympathize. I still remember how embarrassed I was that the non-believer's houses were safe while the Christian's house was broken into two times. After the first time that the thieves came, I walked around our small compound and prayed, pleading the blood of Jesus and declaring that our house would never be broken into again in the name of Jesus Christ!

About six months went by and one morning my house-help told me that there were some muddy foots steps on the verandah outside our kitchen window. It seemed like someone had walked around the house at night, probably looking to see what was the best way to break into the house. I remember that it was a Tuesday and that was the day that I went for the evening prayer meeting at my local church. That evening I went to the prayer meeting and all my focus was on praying for protection from the thieves that had come into our compound the night before. When I came back home from the prayer meeting, I took some anointing oil and poured it all around the house declaring that it was the Blood of Jesus! I dared any thief to cross that bloodline! I went to sleep confident that, we were protected and that no thief would be able to break into our house. How wrong I was! When we woke up in the morning and came downstairs we found our sitting room in disarray. Cushions were thrown all over the floor and the television was missing! There were muddy shoe prints all over the kitchen floor. The thieves had also opened the fridge and drank my milk! I remember thinking, "These thieves actually crossed over the 'Blood of Jesus' and they were not struck down by thunder!" Where were the angelic hosts with flames of fire that I had stationed around my compound? This incident really put a dent in my faith in God.

When our house was broken into in Zambia I began to panic. I knew that something was extremely wrong! Was God trying to punish us for something we had done? My questions to God met with silence. My fervency in prayer started to go down. If God could not protect us then who was going to protect us?

We moved to Mauritania, a West African Muslim country, where we were told that thieves' hands were chopped if they were caught stealing. I relaxed knowing that we were finally safe from thieves. Some missionaries told us that in Mauritania one does not have to lock their doors at night – It was that safe! Wrong again! Just three months after we moved to Mauritania, our house was broken into at night, and our children's bicycles were stolen together with a stereo system and a few electrical appliances. I now knew that there was a curse on us! I now lived in fear and I was no longer the fiery Christian that pleaded the Blood of Jesus and sent Holy Ghost fire on enemies.

When we moved to Senegal after three years in Mauritania, I expected anything to happen to us so when the front side-lights of our car was stolen from the church compound I knew that the next thing that was going to be stolen were my children!

I remember going home that Sunday, locking myself in a room, laying facedown on the floor and weeping. I told God that I was not going to rise up from that floor until He gave me a reason for why we were constantly stolen from. God's answer came clearly and swiftly. This is when He led me to Zechariah chapter 5 concerning the Flying Scroll. *"And he said to me, 'This is the curse that is going out over the whole land; for according to what it says on one side, every thief will be banished, …The Lord Almighty declares, 'I will send it out, and it will enter the house of the thief…It will remain in his house and destroy it, both its timbers and its stones.'"*

When I first read these verses I was in shock! Was God saying that the curse of theft was causing thieves to come to our house because our house was the house of the thief? How could this be? We were not thieves. After some silence I heard the Lord speak to my spirit. Are you really not a thief? How could I argue with God? If God was saying that our house was the house of the thief then it must be true. I decided to humble myself and ask the Holy Spirit to bring to my mind incidences where I had stolen. The first thing I remembered was that the tribe that I came from was considered as cattle thieves. I remembered that there was a song that had been composed about a famous thief from my tribe. Then I remembered how as a child I used to steal money from my dad's coat pocket to buy sweets. On and on I started to remember incidences where I stole from people. When I started working at an international organization there were many grey areas in my life when it came to taking office things. I would take printing paper home to do my own private work. Office pins, and pens belonged to me, and the organization! When I was in university, I once put a hymn- book under my Bible as I was leaving church, so that I could worship God with the hymns that I loved at the hostel as well! I quickly made a connection between the flying scroll and the thieves that constantly broke into our home. I was a born-again believer yet I was a thief!

I got down on my knees and repented for all the incidences that I could remember when I had taken something that did not belong to me. I asked God to forgive me and for Jesus Christ my Advocate to cleanse me with His blood and to plead my case before the Father. I asked God to silence Satan the accuser from accusing me of all the sins of theft that I had committed. I asked God to break the curse of theft from my life, and to stop the Flying Scroll from ever entering our house again. I praise God that that was the last time that our house was broken into in the night, and that was nineteen years ago!

STEALING

Stealing brings a terrible curse on the house of the thief. I learnt this lesson the hard way and pray that somebody reading this book will learn from my mistake and turn away from stealing before the Flying Scroll destroys their house, both its timbers and the stones! The principle here is that the thief will also be stolen from. Proverbs 26:2 tells us that, *"...An undeserved curse does not come to rest."* If you find that you are constantly stolen from, or that you are constantly losing things, or that you are constantly having to repair your things that keep breaking down, then there is a curse of theft on you. The Flying Scroll is finding room to settle on you!

Exodus 20:15, is a very short verse of the Bible. It simply says, *"You shall not steal."*

What is stealing? It is taking anything that does not belong to you – Anything! Many times we take things that do not belong to us and we take it very lightly. It may pay great dividends if we walked through our house and removed everything that did not belong to us and gave them back to the people that they belong to. My greatest culprit was my bookshelf. There were lots of books that I had borrowed but never returned. They had stayed on my bookshelf for so long that I even started to imagine where I had bought them! The Bible says, *"Give and it will be given to you."* –Luke 6:38

I say, "Steal and it will be stolen from you. For in the same way the you steal, someone will also steal from you!" The Flying Scroll does not play games. The first part of Psalm 62:10 says, *"Do not trust in extortion or take pride in stolen goods..."*

DISHONEST MONEY

Unfortunately there are many countries in Africa where a lot of dishonest money is in circulation. Corruption is the order of the day and people bribe their way into anything that they want. I remember that when our family lived in West Africa we encountered a lot of people whose main preoccupation was how to swindle their fellow men out of their hard-earned money. They were called "419". One reformed "419er" told me how they would steal people's credit cards online and use the cards to buy expensive things for themseves. Proverbs 13:11 says, *"Dishonest money dwindles away, but he who gathers little by little makes it grow."* I once saw a documentary on how Policemen get bribes from motorists on the highway. It was said that the traffic policemen had a quota of bribes that their bosses back in the office expected to get from them every day. So traffic offenses continued to be violated by motorists because they knew that they would simply bribe their way out of going to court or paying hefty fines. The interesting thing that I noted was that although some policemen would get an equivalent of $5,000 a day, their lives did not improve and they continued to be poor! Any money that we get in a dishonest way makes us a thief, and a candidate for the Flying Scroll.

DISHONEST SCALES

Leviticus 19:35-36 says, *"Do not use dishonest standards when measuring length, weight or quantity. Use honest weights and honest scales..."* This verse is mainly talking to business people. It is very tempting for business people, especially during the low periods when the business in not bringing in as much money as it should, to be dishonest. There was a time when I was a seamstress (I made my own clothes). I would buy fabrics and sew them into dresses. There would be times when the person measuring the fabric would stretch it as they were cutting it. What that did was that one ended up getting less fabric than they paid for. That is stealing. There are also business people who put stones at the bottom of a container, so that when they put their potatoes, the container looks full, so that you end up buying less potatoes for the price that you have paid for. That is stealing. I remember a butchery that I went to, to buy mince-meat. At one point when the man was weighing out the meat for me, he stood in front of me so that I could not see the meat that he was weighing. He then moved aside and I saw that the weight was correct and that there was no cause for alarm. To my dismay, when I got home I realized that the butcher had sneaked in some rotten meat at the time when he blocked me from seeing what he was doing. That is stealing. Apart from those that use dishonest scales, there are others who make exorbitant interest when they sell their goods. There is a warning for those who make exorbitant interests. *"He who increases his wealth by exorbitant interest amasses it for another, who will be kind to the poor."* Charging an equivalent of $25 for something that I acquired for $2 is dishonest.

NOT PAYING OUR WORKERS

Who is a worker? He or she is someone who gives us services in return for pay. When a person owns a company and has workers, he or she is duty-bound to pay them for the services that they offer him or her. There are employers who, when the company is not doing well, will not pay their workers and justify their actions by saying that they have no money. Luke 10:7 tell us that a worker is worthy of their wages. God is deeply concerned that we pay those who work for us, their rightful due. In many homes in Africa there are "house girls" and "house boys". Their sole purpose is to live with a particular family and do all the work that pertains to the smooth running of the home. In many cases the mothers of the home are career women who leave in the morning and come back in the evening. If the home has small children, then the house girl will bathe the kids, cook their food, feed them, wash clothes, iron them and clean the house. Many of these house workers wake up very early in the morning to prepare breakfast and sleep late at night. Unfortunately many of these workers are mistreated by their employers and in many cases are not paid their rightful dues and many times, not paid on time. What does the Bible say concerning how many people treat their workers? *"Look! The wages you failed to pay the workmen who mowed your fields are crying out against you. The cries of the harvesters, have reached the ears of the Lord Almighty."* – Romans 13:8. When we do not pay our workers, we are stealing from them, and the Flying Scroll is just around the corner! Who can imagine that the cries of some poor workers on a farm can reach the ears of the Lord Almighty?

NOT PAYING OUR DEBTS

Another vice that is responsible for releasing the Flying Scroll, is not paying our debts. Every human being has a divine debt, and this is the debt to love our fellowman. Romans 13:8 says, *Let no debt remain outstanding except the debt to love one another, for he who loves his fellowman has fulfilled the law."* There is nothing inherently wrong with borrowing something from a friend when we are in need. However, borrowing requires that we honor our promise to pay back whatever we borrowed within the time frame that we promised our friend to pay it back. Many wonderful relationships have been ruined because a person borrowed something and did not give back what they borrowed. All of God's children should pray that they reach a point where they give instead of borrowing. The Word of God says that it is more blessed to give than to receive. *"The rich rule over the poor, and the borrower is servant to the lender."* – Proverbs 22:7. God wants His children to be rulers and not to be a servant to lenders. God wants to bless the works of our hands so that we are not debtors, but lenders. The Flying Scroll will knock on the door of the person who does not pay their debts.

NOT PAYING TAXES

In Israel, the tax collectors were some of the most despised people in the society. Jesus, knowing this, said in Matthew 5:46, *"If you love those who love you, what reward will you get? Are not even the tax collectors doing that?"* The implication here is that the tax collectors were such sinful people that if you were doing something that even they did, then there was nothing to show off about. The tax collectors were considered thieves who collected more from the people than they owed, so that they could pocket the difference. Luke 19:2 recounts the story of Zacchaeus, a very short man who climbed a tree so he could see Jesus as He was passing by in the midst of a big crowd. The Bible describes him thus *"... He was a chief tax collector and was wealthy."* Jesus invited Himself to Zaccheaus' home for a meal, and the people murmured saying, *"He has gone to be the guest of a sinner."* After Jesus showed love to this sinful tax collector, he had a change of heart and said to Jesus, *"Look Lord! Here and now I give half of my possessions to the poor. And if I have cheated anybody out of anything, I will pay back four times the amount."* *Zacchaeus was convicted about having cheated people out of taxes.* It would be understandable if people avoided paying taxes because they argued that the tax collectors would eat the money anyway! I am sure that there were many Israelites who probably did not pay taxes and did not feel guilty either. In this scenario, how did Jesus deal with the issue of paying taxes?

Matthew 22:15-22 tells us of an occasion when some Pharisees went to Jesus to try and trap Him concerning the paying of taxes. They probably thought that Jesus would advocate for the non-payment of taxes because of the corrupt system that was in place. Jesus told them. *"Show me the coin used for paying the tax...whose portrait is this and whose inscription?"* – verse 19. They told Him that the portrait and inscription was Caesar's. He then told them, *"Give to Caesar what is Caesar's, and to God what is God's."* On another occasion, some tax collectors approached Peter, Jesus' disciple, and asked him whether Jesus paid the temple tax. Peter's response was, *"Yes he does."* When Peter approached Jesus, He said to him, *"...Go to the lake and throw out your line. Take the first fish you catch; open its mouth and you will find a four-drachma coin. Take it and give it to them for my tax and yours."* Jesus paid His taxes and He expects us to pay our taxes as well. Peter in this story, had not paid his tax but Jesus, in paying Peter's tax as well, was telling Peter indirectly that he needed to pay his taxes.

When we do not pay our taxes, we give opportunity to the devil to accuse us before God, and also the legal right for him to touch our finances. Have you been paying your taxes? Ask Jesus to do a miracle for you as He did when He needed to pay the temple tax for Himself and Peter. Ask Him to bring you that "fish" in whose mouth you will get the money to pay your taxes. God is faithful and will help us obey Him when we have made up our minds that we want to live a life of obedience to His Word.

PRAYER

Heavenly Father, You are the Righteous Judge of all the earth! You stand alone as King of kings and Lord of lords! I now come to Your Courtroom where Satan the Accuser has brought a charge against me. My file says that I am a thief. Your Word says that a curse cannot touch me without a cause. I plead guilty as charged. I am a thief because I have taken things that do not belong to me and I have seen the consequences in my life. I have also not paid my taxes faithfully as Your Word requires of me. People steal from me, they do not pay me back what I have lent to them, I lose things, and many of my things are destroyed and I have to spend money to replace them. These are all signs of the Flying Scroll. I bring repentance for the sin of stealing and I ask that You may have mercy on me and to forgive me! I am sorry Father. Lord Jesus, You are my Righteous Advocate. You have said in 1 John 2:1 that when I sin, You plead my case. Please plead my case before the Father and wash all my sins with Your precious Blood! -The Blood of the everlasting Covenant, the Blood that speaks a better Word than the blood of Abel. Thank You for washing away my sins. Now Father I ask that You would render me "Not Guilty!" in Your Courtroom. Silence the Accuser over my finances. Your Word says that Jesus became poor that I might be rich (2 Corinthians 8:9). I petition that the curse of the Flying Scroll be broken and removed from my house and that I may be rich as Jesus desires it. Thank You for listening to my prayer!

I now take authority and command the evil spirits of **theft, stealing, greed, covetousness, stingy, meanness, dishonesty, bribery, losing things, broken things, lack and poverty,** to come out of me in the name of Jesus Christ! You have no place in me. Come out in the mighty name of Jesus Christ. I am set free right now in the name of Jesus Christ! Breathe out deeply through your mouth until you feel relief. You might yawn or cough or feel sensations in your hands and feet. Do not let that bother you. Be set free today!

DISHONORING GOD AND PARENTS

onor is about appreciating and valuing a person. When I was growing up I did not understand why there were red chairs in the front row of the church that we attended. Why could I not just go and sit there? My little mind did not understand the principle of honor. Those red chairs were for the pastor and the leadership of the church. It was a small way of letting them know that they were appreciated for the work that they do for the house of God. The Apostle Paul told his spiritual son Timothy, *"The elders who direct the affairs of the church well are worthy of double honor, especially those whose work is preaching and teaching."* When we obey the Word of God, we honor God. God wants to be honored, and there are many ways that we can do that. Have you ever thought that giving thanks to God is a way of honoring Him? Psalm 50:23 says, *"He who sacrifices thanks offerings honors me..."* Many times we praise God when our spirit has been lifted up, maybe by a song or testimony. However did you know that when you praise God when you do not feel like it, it honors God? A sacrifice is given to God out of honor and not because we feel like it.

How we deal with poor people is very important to God. The bible tells us that we can honor God by the way we treat poor people. *"He who oppresses the poor shows contempt for their maker, but whoever is kind to the needy honors God."* – Proverbs 14:31. Showing kindness to the needy people around us will release God's blessings upon our life but mistreating the poor will bring a curse and financial lack upon our life.

Another way of honoring God is through our wealth. When the Lord gives us wealth, He expects us to honor Him with it. Proverbs 3:9-10 says, *"Honor the Lord with your possessions, and with the firstfruits of all your increase. So your barns will be filled with plenty, and your vats will overflow with new wine."* For us to have plenty and for us to have overflow, we must first honor God with our wealth and the firstfruits of our increase. Most people understand how to honor God with their wealth through offerings. What many people may not understand is how to honor God with the firstfruits of their increase. What are the firstfruits of our increase? Anytime I am promoted and get an increase in my salary, I should honor God with that increase. I should give the increase of the first month to God. For example, let us assume that my salary has been fifty thousand shillings a month. If I get a promotion in December and my new salary is increased to 60,000 starting January, then I should give God the 10,000 shillings increase for the month of January.

When the Israelites crossed over into the land of Canaan, the first city that they conquered was Jericho. It was the firstfruits of the land that God has promised to them – a land flowing with milk and honey. Joshua decided to honor God with this firstfruits. *"The city and all that is in it are to be devoted to the Lord...All the silver and gold and the articles of bronze and iron are sacred to the Lord and must go into his treasury."* – Joshua 6:17,19. Listen to what God tells Joshua when they attack the second city of Ai. *"You shall do to Ai and its king as you did to Jericho and its king, except that you may carry off their plunder and livestock for yourselves..."* After honoring God with the firstfruits, Israel was now free to enjoy the wealth.

How we treat our first salary when God gives us a job will set the pace for how prosperous we will be in that job. Some years back, a friend of mine told me how when her son got his first job in America, he took the whole of his first month's salary and gave it as an offering to God! I was shocked at the time and did not think her son did a very wise thing. However, soon after that this young man got a promotion and enrolled for a Master's program while working. There was just favor upon favor on his life. Two years later my friend told me that her son won the lottery and got a Green Card! I am convinced that what opened the door to this man's favor was him honoring God with his firstfruits!

CURSED BLESSINGS

How can our blessings be cursed? It seems like a contradiction! How can I be blessed then cursed? Listen to what God told the prophet Malachi. *"If you do not listen, and if you do not set your heart to honor my name, says the Lord Almighty, I will send a curse upon you, and I will curse your blessings! Yes, I have already cursed them because you have not set your heart to honor me."* As we have already said, God wants to be honored and if we do not honor Him, He curses our blessings! This verse is talking about obedience – "If you do not listen." Listening to God brings on a blessing but not listening will bring frustration and lack. What do cursed blessings look like?

1)   God gives you a car and you rejoice because you have been praying for a car for a long time. However, after a short time your car starts to have mechanical problems. Almost every weekend you are at the garage having your car fixed. There are many people whose cars that were supposed to be a blessing have turned out to be a curse!

2)   You have been hoping and praying that the Lord would give you a computer, for a long time. However, you do not have the money to buy it. The company where you work is disposing of its old computers as they upgrade to a newer model. You do not have money to buy a computer from the company but a friend of yours who knows how much you want a computer, surprises you by buying one for you! It is a day of celebration! However after just a month, your computer starts to give you problems. Each time one problem is fixed, another one shows up. Your computer has finally closed down with very important document that you need. What started off as a blessing, has now become a curse.

3)   Your child has just finished high school and gotten a tuition scholarship to go and study in the United States. The visa comes through very easily. You ask your friends to help you raise money for his upkeep and for books. The response is overwhelming, as your friends rally behind you and raise more money than he needs! You see this as a great blessing and thank God as you celebrate. Your son goes to the United States and after a few months, stops picking your calls and does not respond to text messages. You start to panic because this is not the character of your son. Six months go by, no communication from your son. A year goes by, and you actually consider raising money to go to the United States to find out what has happened to your son. A friend who lives in the same state as him writes to you and tells you that he met your son. He has dropped out of school and has joined a company of young people who are drug addicts! Your blessing has turned into a curse!

These three examples are how your blessings can be cursed when you do not listen to God or dishonor Him. Dishonoring God has a dire consequence of poverty, lack, and struggle. Let the Holy Spirit convict you personally of ways that you have dishonored God.

I remember the Holy Spirit once convicting me of not chewing gum in church. When we dishonor God's sanctuary, we dishonor Him as well. The Holy Spirit also convicted me about not cracking jokes about God, or even laughing when someone cracks a joke about Jesus or the Holy Spirit. Let the Holy Spirit be your guide on what honors God and what dishonors Him.

DISHONORING PARENTS

God chose that each one of us should come to this earth through a man and a woman who we call father and mother. These are our parents. God wants us to honor the two people through whom we came to this earth, and without whom we would not exist!

When children are young and still living under the roof of their parents' house, they are supposed to show honor by obeying their parents in the Lord. In Proverbs 22:6 parents are told to train up their children in the ways of the Lord. Children should obey their parents as their parents obey God by training them in His ways. It is for this reason that God gave this command to Moses concerning a rebellious and disobedient child. *"...His father and mother shall take hold of him and bring him to the elders at the gate of his town. They shall say to the elders, 'This son of ours is stubborn and rebellious. He will not obey us. He is a profligate and drunkard' Then all the men of his town shall stone him to death. You must purge the evil from among you. All Israel shall hear of it and be afraid."* – Deuteronomy 21:19-21. Wow! What a harsh sentence! However God knew that a stubborn and rebellious child would later turn into a stubborn and rebellious adult. This rebellious child would later on worship other gods in rebellion to God's laws! I am sure that many Israelite parents suffered in silence under stubborn and rebellious children because they did not want their children stoned to death. Children whose parents protected their stubbornness and rebellion still stood out in the community because even if they escaped punishment from the community, they could not escape punishment from disobeying the Law. One of the Ten Commandments said, *"Honor your father and mother, as the Lord your God has commanded you, so that you may live long and that it may go well with you in the land the Lord your God is giving you."* – Deuteronomy 5:16. The Word of God says that it will not go well with anyone who dishonors father and mother. It also says that they will not live for long. I am sure that in the Israelite camp, it was easy to pick out the people who had dishonored their parents even if their parents, out of love for them, did not bring them to the elders at the gate of their town. Their lives were not prosperous. Calamity followed their lives, and they died young.

The Apostle Paul, in teaching about the relationship between children and parents also quoted from Deuteronomy 5:6 *"Children, obey your parents in the Lord for this is right. 'Honor your father and mother' – which is the first commandment with a promise – 'that it may go well with you and that you may enjoy long life on the earth.'"* – Ephesians 6:1-3. There is a promise for us when we honor our parents. We are promised that it will go well with us and that we will enjoy long life here on earth. In verse four of this chapter, we see a caution to fathers. *"Fathers, do not exasperate your children; instead, bring them up in the training and instruction of the Lord."* When we exasperate our children, we may push them to dishonor us whereby it does not go well with them. The sad thing is that even when a parent does something to their child that pushes that child to dishonor them, punishment will still come on the child. No loving parent is at peace when it does not go well with their child. Parents do themselves a favor by not doing anything that will cause their child to dishonor them.

We can clearly see how there may be people who are suffering lack and poverty because they did not, or are not honoring their father and mother. May be both your parents are no longer living, yet you know that you did not honor them. It is still not too late to repent and overturn the curse into a blessing. Just sincerely pray the prayer at the end of this chapter.

PRAYER

Heavenly Father, You have told us in your Word that we should honor you and our parents. As I look back Lord I can see many incidences where I dishonored my parents. There are also incidences where I have dishonored You. I have not honored you with my possessions and with the firstfruits of all my possessions. Satan has accused me to you as the Righteous Judge, and I accept that I am guilty as charged! I deserve the poverty and lack in my life because of these sins that I have not yet repented of. I bring repentance for the sin of dishonoring You and my parents. Please forgive me. I ask for mercy. Lord Jesus, You are my Advocate who pleads my case before the Father. I ask you to wash away my sins with Your Blood, which was shed on the Cross of Calvary for me. Thank You for cleansing me with Your Blood. Now Heavenly Father and my Righteous Judge, I ask you to render me not guilty of these sins. Silence the Accuser on my behalf. I now petition that the legal right that Satan has to affect my finances be taken from him. May I walk in the prosperity that You have ordained for me. I now take authority and command the spirits of **dishonor of parents, dishonor of God, stubbornness, rebellion, pride, arrogance, misplaced boldness, poverty, lack and struggle** to leave me now in the name of Jesus Christ! You have no more right to be here. Be gone in Jesus name! Now breathe out through your mouth several times until you feel relief. You might yawn or cough or feel sensations in you hands and feet. He who the Son sets free is free indeed! I turn every financial curse into a blessing in the mighty name of Jesus Christ! He who the Son sets free is free indeed! – AMEN!

CHAPTER

9

UNDERSTANDING THE PRINCIPLE OF TITHING

The first time that we hear about tithe being mentioned in the Bible is Leviticus 27:30, although it was not the first time that ten percent was being given as an offering. Lot, Abram's nephew had gone to live in Sodom. Four kings ganged up together and went to war against Sodom and Gomorrah. When Sodom was captured, Lot and his family were also captured. When Abram heard that his nephew Lot had also been captured, he gathered his men together and went to rescue his nephew. Abram defeated the kings and rescued his nephew and also got a lot of plunder. Melchizedek the priest of God in Sodom came to meet Abram, and Abram offered him ten percent of all that he had. Later on when Jacob was running away from his brother Esau who wanted to kill him, he had an encounter with God, and God reminded him of the promise He had made to Abraham. Jacob made a vow to God. *"...And of all the you give me I will give you a tenth."* – Genesis 28:22. I do not know why both Abram and Jacob gave and vowed to give ten percent. This was way before God commanded the Israelites to give ten percent as tithe.

Before God asked the Israelites to give ten percent of their produce as an offering, God had told Moses that certain parts of the animal brought as an offering to God was allotted to the priests (Aaron and his sons). From the grain offering, some of it was also to be given to the priests. However as the number of priests began to grow, God introduced tithe and set it at ten percent. *"A tithe of everything from the land, whether grain from the soil or fruit from the trees, belongs to the Lord; it is holy to the Lord...The entire herd of the herd and flock – every tenth animal that passes under the shepherd's rod – will be holy to the Lord."* Why did God want the Israelites to bring in the tithe? God's concern was mainly that the priests be taken care of because the priests had no inheritance in Israel. *"Bring the whole tithe into the storehouse, that there may be food in my house..."* – Malachi 3:10. The Levites were the only Israelites called as priests, and they were the ones that God was mainly concerned about. Why was God concerned about the priests? Listen to what God said to Aaron, *"You will have no inheritance in their land, nor will you have any share among them; I am your share and your inheritance among the Israelites."* While the different tribes of Israelite were being given portions of land, no inheritance was given to the Levites. They were also supposed to do the work in the temple daily, so they would not have had any time to till their land. If God left it to the Israelites to take care of the Levites, they would have been in lack all the time because of the hardness on man's heart. It is very probable that the Israelites would not have provided adequately for the priests. God had to set a rule that would ensure that the Levites were taken care of and so He commanded the Israelites to bring ten percent of everything that they produced, to the Levites. *"I give all the Levites all the tithes in Israel as their inheritance in return for the work they do while serving at the Tent of Meeting."* – Numbers 18:21. In Deuteronomy 12:19 God warned the Israelites sternly, *"Be careful not to neglect the Levites as long as you live in your land."*

With this background we can now understand why God was so upset with the Israelites in Malachi 3:8-9. He called them robbers for not bringing the whole tithe to the storehouse and told them that the whole nation of them was under a curse! There was no food in God's house for the Levites! This was because they were not bringing the whole tithe. Some of them would probably bring half (five percent) meaning to bring fifteen percent next time. God was not amused! However, God decided to give them an incentive for bringing in the whole tithe. *"Test me in this, says the Lord Almighty, and see if I will not throw open the floodgates of heaven and pour out so much blessing that you will not have room enough for it. I will prevent pests from devouring your crops, and the vines in your fields will not cast their fruit...Then all the nations will call you blessed, for yours will be a delightful land, says the Lord Almighty."* We need to remember that the Israelites did not have the Holy Spirit to convict them to tithe. You and I, if we are believers in Jesus Christ, have the Holy Spirit to convict us. We do not need to be coerced to tithe. However, even with the Holy Spirit indwelling us, many people still find it hard to tithe.

Why do many Believers find it hard to tithe? It is because tithing brings us back to the law, and fulfilling the law does not bring joy! Not tithing, releases a curse on Believers, in the same way that worshiping another god also releases a curse. In Deuteronomy 27:15-26 are thirteen curses that will come on people who do various things. Deuteronomy 28:15-68 has more curses that are supposed to fall on people who worship other gods. However, Galatians 3:13 tells us that Jesus redeemed us from the curse of the law and became a curse for us when He died on the Cross of Calvary! Did He also redeem us from the curse that comes from not tithing? Yes He did! Jesus became a curse for us the same way that He became sin for us. *"God made him who had no sin to be sin for us, so that in him, we might become the righteousness of God."* – 2 Corinthians 5:21. Praise God that Jesus died for the sins of the whole world! However, is everybody in the whole world saved? No! Although Jesus died for the sins of the whole world we must appropriate what He did on the Cross. In the same way, although Jesus became my "curse of not tithing", I must appropriate what He did on the Cross so that the curse does not touch me when I do not tithe! We deal with the curse in the same way that we deal with sin. With sin I must:

1) Accept that I am a sinner.
2) Believe that Jesus Christ became my sin.
3) Repent.
4) Confess (Romans 10:9-10).

In the same way I can also deal with the curse of not tithing and declare and confess it broken through the finished work of the Cross of Calvary.

FROM TITHER TO GIVER

In the New Testament we encounter a principle that encourages us to be givers. In 2 Corinthians 9:6 we are told, *"Remember this: Whoever sows sparingly will also reap sparingly, and whoever sows generously will also reap generously."* We are told here that what we reap is in direct proportion to what we sow. Little sowing, little harvest, and big sowing, big harvest! I have realized that it is only within the Christian circles that giving ten percent is considered generous enough to open the windows of heaven, and pour out such a blessing that you will not know where to put it.

Recently while teaching on financial curses I asked my audience how many people tithed regularly. Many hands went up. Then I asked, how many of the people whose hands were up, had experienced the windows of heaven opening and pouring out such a blessing that they did not know where to put it. All the hands went down! Why is it that people tithe regularly yet the blessings that are promised when we tithe are not manifested in their live? Something is wrong. Why is it that even if we keep our side of the bargain, God does not seem to keep His side of the bargain? It is because God moved away from tithing and entered into a new covenant of giving when Jesus died on the Cross of Calvary. "God so loved the world that **He gave** his only Son." God gave generously and in the new dispensation we also must give generously in order to reap generously! Tithing is not generous and so it cannot produce a manifestation of abundance. The good measure that is pressed down, shaken together and running over that is spoken of in Luke 6:38 can only be received through our generosity and not by giving ten percent! Mark 4:24 says, *"With the measure you use, it will be measured to you..."*

Tithing robs us of God's blessing, because it encourages us to give very little. Also once a person has tithed, they often think that they have done their duty and need not give anymore. After giving their tithe of ten percent, most people sit back and wait for the windows of heaven to open, much to the disappointment of the many people, as I saw manifested in the meeting where I was teaching. Let us graduate from being tithers, to being givers.

Another principle that we see in the Word of God is seen in 2 Corinthians 9:7 which says, *"Each man should give what he has decided in his heart to give, not reluctantly or under compulsion, for God loves a cheerful giver."* Tithing does not accord us the opportunity to decide what to give. We don't decide how much tithe to give. God told the Israelites to give ten percent, no more and no less. They were forced to give the tithe or come under a curse! Thank God that when we are givers, we do not have to fear coming under a curse. We will simply reap much or little depending on how much we have sowed. The Bible tells us that God loves a cheerful giver. It is hard to give cheerfully when there is a threat of a curse hanging over our heads.

2 Corinthians 9:8 is a promise to us that when we are generous givers, *"...God is able to make all grace abound to you, so that in*

all things at all times, having all the you need, you will abound in every good work. There are many people who tithe regularly but are still struggling under a yoke of poverty. Givers however, are promised that in all things, at all times, they will have everything that they need.

As givers we are supposed to be aware of the needs around us and allow God to use us to meet those needs 1 John 3:17 says, *"If anyone has material possessions and sees his brother in need but has no pity on him, how can the love of God be in him?"* Love manifests itself through meeting the needs of the people around me through giving. Two passages of Scripture from the Book of Psalm say:

1)   *"A generous man will himself be blessed, for he shares his food with the poor."* – Proverbs 22:9

2)   *"He who gives to the poor will lack nothing, but he who closes his eyes to them receives many curses."* – Proverbs 28:27.

PRAYER

Heavenly Father, I thank you for what You have taught me from your Word concerning tithing. I have been under a curse for not tithing regularly. Each time I have missed a month of tithing I have felt very guilty. I have made promises to tithe but have not kept them. Please forgive me. Lord Jesus I ask You to cleanse me in Your Blood. I thank you that Jesus Christ redeemed me from the curse of the law by becoming a curse for me. Today I break the curse of not tithing and I nail it to the Cross of Calvary. From today I want to be a giver. Help me be generous not only because I want something back in return, but because I genuinely care about the needy people around me. Father, as a Righteous Judge, remove the curse of not tithing from me and render me not guilty. Silence the Accuser on my behalf. Now I take authority and command every spirit that has been attacking my finances to go in Jesus name! **Spirits of Poverty, the devourer, pests, financial lack, no promotion, no favor,** come out in the name of Jesus Christ! You have no more room here! Be gone in the name of Jesus Christ! Breathe out through your mouth until you feel relief. You might yawn or cough or feel sensations in you hands and feet. I am set free in the name of Jesus! He who the Son sets free is free indeed. I declare that I am entering into my prosperity. As the Lord blesses me, I will also use my wealth to bless other people.

SOWING IN BAD SOIL

nyone who sows in bad soil should not expect a harvest. Jesus gave the parable of "The Sower" in Mark chapter 4 and in Matthew chapter thirteen. Jesus said that the sower went out to sow seed. For a long time I thought that sowing seed meant giving money. However Mark 4:14, in Jesus' explanation of the meaning of this parable, He said that the **farmer sows the Word**. When His disciples asked Jesus why He spoke in parables, He told them, *"The knowledge of the secrets of the kingdom of heaven has been given to you, but not to them."* – Matthew 13:11. This verse implies that the Kingdom of heaven has secrets, the knowledge of which, God gives to His children! That means that, this parable had secrets, that hearers would not understand just by listening and hearing. Jesus went on to remind them of the prophecy of Isaiah that said, *"...You will be ever hearing but never understanding..."* This leads me to a very serious realization which means that one could be teaching people over and over again about something that they are hearing but not understanding! In Jesus' teaching, He always used parables (Matthew 13:34). *"So was fulfilled what was spoken through the prophet: 'I will open my mouth in parables, I will utter things hidden since the creation of the world."* – Matthew 13:35. In Jesus' parables are hidden things! Any time we come across a parable of Jesus, we should ask the Holy spirit to reveal to us the meaning of it otherwise we may be among the ones that are *"...Ever hearing but never understanding..."* – Matthew 13:14. The reason that Jesus gave for this state of affairs was because, *"...This people's heart has become calloused..."* – Matthew 13:15. To be calloused is to have an area or areas of hardened skin. For example, most guitar players have calloused finger -tips where they have pressed the thin guitar strings over and over again. I learnt how to play the guitar when I was quite young and at the time, each time I tried to play a chord by pressing on the strings, I would feel pain on my finger-tips. However, after a while of constantly playing the guitar, the pain became less and less. After a while, my finger- tips hardened and I no longer felt pain when I played the guitar. Calloused skin has little or no sensation or feeling. In the same way, a soft heart is sensitive and has feeling while a calloused heart has very little sensitivity or feeling. In this context, Jesus was saying that although somebody with a calloused heart hears a message over and over, it does not touch them or affect their feelings. They have lost sensitivity.

How does a person's heart become calloused? A person that has been hurt over and over again will develop a calloused heart. It is the heart's way of protecting itself from pain. One can also sin over and over again to the point that their heart is calloused. They will reach a point where sinning does not affect them any longer. They will eventually sin without feeling guilty! A child that is lied to over and over again by the people around them, especially by their parents, will reach a point of having such a calloused heart that anything that they hear, they consider a lie!

Having understood what having a calloused heart is, let us go back to the parable of the sower. Jesus said that the Word that was sown encountered four different conditions of the heart.

1)   The first seed fell along the path, and the birds came and ate it up. Although this person heard the word, it did not produce

any effect in his life. Although he or she heard a teaching on how to break financial curses, his financial situation did not change. Jesus explained this first situation thus, *"When anyone hears the message about the kingdom and does not understand it, the evil one comes and snatches away what was sown in his heart."* – Matthew 13:19. Here the evil one is equated to birds. A person may not understand the Word of God for many reasons, but in this case, Jesus says that the person did not understand the Word preached to him because of the condition of his heart. The Word fell on a calloused and hardened heart. The Word may have come with power, but was unable to penetrate the hearer's heart. This person may have suffered so much in life that they did not understand how anything could take away their suffering. This explanation tells us how important it is for a person to understand what we teach and preach. If they do not understand it, Satan will come and snatch away what was sown in their heart. This seed fell on bad soil and produced nothing!

2) The second example that Jesus gave was of seed that fell on rocky places. *"...Where it did not have much soil. It sprang up quickly, because the soil was shallow. But when the sun came up, the plants were scorched, and they withered because they had no root."* This second example may refer to baby Christians who have recently received the Lord Jesus Christ in their lives. They were brought up as Christians and have not grown up hearing the Word. They are excited and eager to live for Christ but have very little knowledge of the Word. Listen to how Jesus describes them. *"The one who received the word that fell on rocky places is the man who hears the Word and immediately receives it with joy. But since he has no root, he lasts only a short time. When trouble and persecution comes because of the word, he quickly falls away.* This person also

has a hard and calloused heart. He grew up doing things his own way and no one corrected him. He is not rooted in the Word of God. He may be easily blown away by every wind of doctrine. He cannot stand upon what he believes. If somebody comes and challenges what he believes in, he quickly moves from his position. He may hear the teaching on how to break financial curses and believe it only as long as somebody else does not come and challenge his belief. Although he has heard and quickly received the teaching, he will bear no fruit.

3)   The third example is of seed that fell among thorns, which grew up and choked the plants. Hebrews 6:8 tells us *"But land that produces thorns and thistles is worthless and is in danger of being cursed. In the end it will be burned."* This Hebrews passage seems to be talking of thorns as those that do not believe in God. Jesus also explained the meaning of the seed that fell among thorns. *"The one who received the seed that fell among thorns is the man who hears the word, but the worries of this life and the deceitfulness of wealth choke it, making it unfruitful."* This third group is the believer who lives in close contact with worldly people. Their close friends are not believers. Their friends are people who are immersed in the worries of this life and spend their lives seeking after wealth. This third group has a heart that is calloused because of always hearing the philosophies of the world. It is this third group that 1 John 2:15-16 addresses. *"Do not love the world or the things which are in the world. If anyone loves the world, the love for the Father is not in him. For everything in the world – the cravings of sinful man, the lust of the eyes and the boasting of what he has and does – comes not from the Father but from the world."* This third group, also have calloused and hard hearts, which have been influenced by the way the world thinks. Although they may hear a message on

how to break financial curses, it does not make sense to them because they have believed in what the world says about how to make wealth. Psalm 1:1-2 says *"Blessed is the man who does not stand in the counsel of the wicked, or stand in the way of sinners or sit in the seat of mockers, but his delight is in the law of the Lord and on his law he meditates day and night."* This third group will hear the Word but the Word will not make them financially successful.

4) The final seed that the parable of the sower talks about is the seed that fell on good soil where it produced a crop! All four groups of people sat in the same meeting but only one group produced a crop! This is the group of people whose hearts were not calloused or hardened. The Bible exhorts parents to bring up their children in the ways of the Lord so that when they grow up they will not depart from it. When parents do this, their children grow up with a soft heart towards the Word of God. Sowing in bad soil, then, is preaching or teaching the Word of God to people whose hearts are calloused. It is interesting to note that even the good soil did not produce a hundred percent for all the hearers. Some people reaped only thirty percent and others, sixty. Depending on how much a person has been immersed in the things of God, to the same extent he will reap a harvest. This fourth group of people also heard the message on breaking financial curses, but not everybody reaped the same amount from the teaching. Our aim should be to reap a hundred percent from the teachings that we hear. How does a person have a soft heart towards the things of God? The first and most important thing is prayer. We need to constantly pray that God enlightens the eyes of our heart (Ephesians 1:18). Receiving from God is a heart issue. We need to ask the Holy Spirit to soften our hearts. Secondly, as we constantly read the Word of God, we become acquainted

with His ways and His character. This will help us trust and believe what God tells us from His Word. Faith is needed in order to believe God, and it comes from hearing and continuing to hear the Word of God.

PRAYER

Heavenly Father, thank you for teaching me about how the condition of my heart will determine how much I understand and receive from Your precious Word. Forgive me for not reading enough of Your Word so that my heart can be softened. Also forgive me for keeping company with people who do not care for the things of God and getting my counsel from them. Help me make it a priority to attend Bible studies and home groups where I can fellowship with people of like mind. I have allowed myself to be immersed in the things of this world. Please forgive me. I pray that my heart would be good soil so that anytime the Word is sown there, it will produce a one hundred percent crop! I now take authority as a servant of the living God and kick out the spirits of; **fear of persecution, man- pleasing, misunderstanding the Word, worry, seeking wealth, poverty, lack, and struggling**. Leave me now in the name of Jesus Christ! You have no place in my life. Breathe out through your mouth until you feel relief. You might yawn or cough or feel sensations in you hands and feet. He who the Son sets free is free indeed! He who the Son sets free is free indeed!

CHAPTER
11

UNDERSTANDING GOD'S FAVOR

Many times people tell me that they are fasting and trusting God for a certain amount of money. This money could be capital to start a business, to buy a house, or even for school fees. They usually have given God a time line within which the money should come. This time line often corresponds to how soon they want to start the business; How long the house they want to buy will be on the market, before somebody else buys it; When school is opening. Because of the time line, there is usually a sense of desperation and anxiety. Should the time line pass without any sign of the money most people become disappointed with God. They fasted, prayed and believed, but God did not come through for them. Once God has failed them, they often opt for plan 'B', which is to get someone to borrow the money from. This is how people get into debt, which then becomes like a chain around their necks.

Once we understand that when we need something, getting money is not the only way through which God will give it to us, we will stop asking God for money. What then should we ask God for? When we have needs - start a business, own a house, or school fees – we should ask God to meet that need and let Him decide how He will meet it. If it is God that is laying it on my heart to start a business, then He will make provision for me to start that business.

The first thing that God does is that we start to have favor with the people that are involved in us starting a business. For example if I want to start a Kindergarten, God may cause me to unexpectedly meet someone who has been running a Kindergarten and is looking for someone to sell the business to. God may cause him or her to trust me so much that they sell the business to me and ask me to pay them in installments instead of paying them all the money at once. That is called God's favor. In Luke 2:52 we are told, *"And Jesus grew in wisdom and stature, and in favor with God and men."* It is perfectly in line for us to pray to have favor with God and men. Once a person becomes a Believer then they have favor with God. Once we have favor with God, He will cause us to have favor with men. A friend of mine recently told me how she and her husband wanted to buy a car. They eventually found a beautiful car that they wanted to buy. The car owner who they had not known previously told them that he did not know why he was doing this because he had never done it before, but they could have the car and pay him later. That is called God's favor. It is not only money that can get us the things that we need. A time comes, when we are able to "buy" without money!

Isaiah 55:1 says, *"...And you who have no money, come, buy wine and milk without money and without cost."* How can we buy without money? Favor can buy us more than money can buy. At a recent seminar where I was teaching on Breaking Financial Curses, a lady gave a testimony of how God had given her favor with the director of the special- school that her autistic child attended. She told us that the director waived school fees for a whole term, at a time when they had no money. A different person also gave a testimony of how he was called to go to a college to study but had no money to pay for tuition. He told us how a few friends got together and decide to contribute towards his school fees. That is called God's favor. He paid for his tuition *"without money and without cost."* When God wants to show us favor, He will touch somebody's heart that will show us favor.

Jesus told a parable in Matthew 20:1-16, telling His disciples that the Kingdom of heaven was like a land owner who went out early in the morning to hire men to work in his vineyard. He agreed to pay them a denarius for the day and sent them into his vineyard. The landowner went out again at the third, six, and ninth hour of the day and each time he found men sitting around hoping for work, with no one hiring them. Each time he hired them, saying, *"You also go and work in my vineyard, and I will pay you whatever is right"* (verse 4). At the eleventh hour, just one hour before the end of the work -day, the landowner hired the last lot of men. When evening came the landowner told his foreman to call in the workers and pay each of them their wages beginning with those who had only worked for one hour. They were given a denarius each. All the workers were given a denarius, which aroused the wrath of the workers who had worked the whole day for twelve hours! They expected that if the people who had worked for one hour got a denarius then they would get 12 denarii! Listen to what the landowner said. *"Don't I have the right to do what I want with my own money? Or are you envious because I am generous?"* (verse 15). Favor earned the men who worked for just one hour, the same amount as those who had worked for twelve hours! That is what the kingdom of God is like! God will favor whomever He chooses. We cannot work for favor, and so it cannot be earned. When the Israelites were leaving Egypt, they "bought" silver, gold and clothing without money and without cost! The Bible tells us that, *"The Lord had made the Egyptians favorably disposed toward the people. And they gave then whatever they asked for..."* God can make anyone favorably disposed towards me so that they give me whatever I ask for. So we should not pray for money but for favor. The Lord is well able to meet our needs and He does not need money to do it! My prayer should not be for what God should give me. This kind of prayer assumes that I know what I need. God is the one who knows what I need. My prayer should be, Lord meet this need that I have. It will then be God's prerogative how He meets the need. He may choose to give me money or cause someone else to give me what I need. Favor is more powerful than money!

Why do people often ask for money? It is because money is a status symbol in many communities. Money makes us feel rich, and when we do not have it we feel poor. Once we see money as the answer to all our problems we will pursue it even to the detriment of our own souls! The bible says, that the **love of money** is the root of all evil. Let us learn to ask God for favor.

We should never fast so that God gives us money. If God has decided that He will not give us the money that we are asking for because He has a different plan for our lives, no amount of fasting will release that money from His hands. We cannot manipulate God through fasting. Fasting is meant to soften our hearts so that we can hear God more clearly concerning a particular issue.

PRAYER

Heavenly Father, I thank you for teaching me about Your favor. I thank you that Your favor is upon my life because of the finished work of the cross of Calvary. You showed me undeserved favor when Jesus died for me. *"...While we were still sinners, Christ died for us."* –Romans 5:8. What a wonderful God You are! I come to Your Supreme Court where You are the Righteous Judge and ask for forgiveness for assuming that I know what I need and that it is money that will get it for me. Today I know that what I need is just Your favor. You have told me in the Word that you know what I need. I bring to You all my needs right now. You have told me in 2 Peter 1:3 that you have already given me everything I need for life. Help me put my trust in the fact that You are the One who knows how to manifest them in my life. Forgive me for worry and anxiety. Also forgive me for trying to manipulate You through fasting. Let Your favor manifest powerfully in my life. Lord Jesus please wash me in Your precious blood. Cleanse me so that I am white as snow. I now thank you for cleansing me, redeeming me and justifying me through Your blood! I take authority as a child of God and command every spirit of **worry, anxiety, apprehension, self-sufficiency, love of money, fear of poverty, lack, struggling, stagnation, covetousness, no faith, no favor, no promotion, no money, debt, and fear** to leave me now in the name of Jesus Christ! You have no right to be here! Go in the name of Jesus! Breathe out through your mouth until you feel relief. You might yawn or cough or feel sensations in you hands and feet. He who the Son sets free is free indeed!

CHAPTER 12

A WARNING ABOUT WEALTH

I think I am right to assume that anyone who has reached the level of wealth that they are happy with, will not pick up to read, a book with the title, "BREAKING FINANCIAL CURSES". So this warning is for those of us who are still aspiring to reach the level of prosperity that Jesus died on the cross for us to have! It is God's will that His child live in prosperity with no lack in their lives. However, the Bible is replete with warnings to the rich and wealthy.

OLD TESTAMENT WARNINGS

Although the Book of Job is somewhere in the middle of the Bible just before the Book of Psalm, scholars agree that it is the oldest book of the Bible. The first warning that the Bible gives us about wealth in the Old Testament is found as we read the familiar story of Job. Job was the richest man in the East and the magnitude of his vast wealth is recounted in verse two of the first chapter. Yet a few verses later when he has lost all his wealth Job says, *"Naked I came from my mother's womb and naked I will depart."* – Job 1:20. Job tasted plenty and also experienced lack and suffering. Later on towards the end of the Book he says that God shows no partiality to princes, *"...And does not favor the rich over the poor, for they are all the work of his hands."* – Job 34:19. Once Job had come to this realization, God made him twice as rich as he was before. Although God wants us to be rich, He wants us to have the right attitude towards wealth and riches.

After Job we meet king Solomon. The Bible describes king Solomon as greater in riches than all the other kings of the earth. When God told this king to ask for anything that he wanted and God would give it to him, he asked for wisdom to govern the people of God (1 Kings 3:4-9). God could have given him wisdom and left it at that. However God made him the richest king that ever lived! What did Solomon think of his wealth and riches? Did the riches bring him satisfaction? Solomon says in the Book of Ecclesiastes 5: 10. *"Whoever has money never has money enough; whoever loves wealth is never satisfied with his income. This too is meaningless."* The wisest man on the face of the earth must have known what he was talking about! Finally Solomon realized that *"Moreover, when God gives any man wealth and possessions, and enables him to enjoy them, to accept his lot and be happy in his work – this is a gift from God."* – Ecclesiastes 5:19. Wealth that is a gift from God will bring peace and joy. However king Solomon also says that he has seen a grievous evil under the sun: *"...Wealth hoarded to the harm of its owner."* – Ecclesiastes 5:13. Finally king Solomon gives us a final word. *"The sleep of a laborer is sweet, whether he eats little or much, but the abundance of a rich man permits him no sleep."*

The Bible describes King David as a man after God's heart. God also gave king David great wealth. Before he died he provided for his son Solomon all the materials that he would need to build a magnificent temple for God. *"...He overlaid the inside with pure gold, and he also overlaid the altar of cedar. Solomon covered the inside of the temple with pure gold, and he extended gold chains across the front of the inner sanctuary, which was overlaid with gold. So he overlaid the whole interior with gold. He also overlaid with gold the altar that belonged to the inner sanctuary."* That was a lot of gold that king David provided for his son to build the temple. Although king David was extremely wealthy, he also gave a warning to the rich. *"Do not be overawed when a man grows rich, when the splendor of his house increases; for he will take nothing with him when he dies, his splendor will not descend with him."* No wonder God gave king David so much wealth. He did not allow his wealth to turn his heart away from God and he realized that wealth was only for this earth!

NEW TESTAMENT WARNINGS

Although Jesus was rich He chose to be poor so that you and I can be rich (2 Corinthians 8:9). Jesus wants us to be rich to that extent! In Psalm 50:12 *"for the world is mine and all that is in it."* Although Jesus wants us to be rich, He also has a warning for us. *"Watch out! Be on your guard against all kinds of greed; a man's life does not consist in the abundance of his possessions."* If a man's life does not consist in the abundance of his wealth, then what does a man's life consist of? I believe that a man's life consists of to what extend he accomplishes his purpose here on earth. Wealth is supposed to be used to help us accomplish the purpose for which God created us! Psalm 139:16 *"All the days ordained for me were written in your book before one of them came to be."* We all have a book of destiny and purpose. Riches will help me go where I am supposed to go, do what I am supposed to do and help those I am supposed to help, before I pack up and go back to God to give an account of how I accomplished my purpose while on mission here on earth. We are here as ambassadors to bring the government of the "country" that sent us. Every ambassador needs wealth. Jesus' warning was against all kinds of greed. Once we understand our purpose then there is no room for greed! Acts 13:36 tells us that *"... When David had served God's purpose in his own generation, he fell asleep; he was buried with his fathers and his body decayed."* Whatever wealth David had, he used to accomplish God's purpose in his own generation. How are you using your wealth?

In Luke 12:16-21 Jesus told His disciples the parable of the rich fool. Let us see, where this rich man 'lost the way'. *"The ground of a certain rich man produced a good crop. He thought to himself, 'What shall I do? I have no place to store my crops (verse 16)."* A good crop comes from God who gives us rain. At this point he had a genuine problem. He had no place to store his blessing. *"Then he said, this is what I will do. I will tear down my barns and build bigger ones, and there I will store all my grain and my goods (verse 18)."* Right here we see common sense. If your current storage place cannot hold your harvest, it makes perfect sense to build a bigger storage space. If this story had ended here, we would have all gone home as happy people! However the story does not end here. The last and final thing that this rich man says is what got him in trouble! *"And I will say to myself, 'You have plenty of good things laid up for many years. Take life easy; eat drink and be merry (verse 19).'"* This is where the problem was! Who, is speaking to who here? It is the spirit man speaking to his soul. The spirit man does not need things. He is spirit and therefore can only access spiritual things. However the spirit man lives in a body that has a soul (mind, emotions, will). The spirit lives forever but the soul and body do not. So the spirit is telling his soul that lives in a temporary body, to take life easy, to eat, drink and be merry. In other words, you have many years ahead of you. Do not worry about anything while here on earth. *"But God said to him, 'You fool! This very night your life will be demanded from you. Then who will get what you have prepared for yourself?"* Who is God talking to? God is talking to the spirit-man. A person can only communicate with God in their spirit. The soul and body cannot communicate with God. God is telling the spirit of this rich man that they are a fool to imagine that they control how long the can live on this earth. It is a reminder of the mortality of the soul. God is telling the spirit-man that that very night, their soul and body will be demanded of them, in death. We cannot afford to live on this earth as though we are here forever. Jesus finally ends the parable by saying, *"This is how it will be with anyone who stores up things for himself, but is not rich toward God."* The fallacy of one storing things for themselves here on earth is that they are going to die and leave those things here on earth. Instead of storing things for ourselves here on earth where we live temporarily in our body, Jesus encouraged His disciples to be more concerned with the condition of their spirit-man – How rich are they toward God? A person that is rich toward God is one who is aware that they are here on earth to accomplish God's purpose for a short time and then leave. They are therefore concerned with how to live a life that is pleasing to God, and how to make sure that they are always walking in the center of God's will.

A final warning that I will talk about is found in Matthew 6:19-21. *"Do not store up for yourselves treasures on earth, where moth and rust destroy, and where thieves break in and steal. But store up for yourselves treasures in heaven, where moth and rust do not destroy, and where thieves do not break in and steal. For where your treasure is, there your heart will be also."* It is obvious how people store up for themselves treasures here on earth where moths have destroyed their treasure and where thieves have broken in and stolen. On the other hand, how do we store up for ourselves treasures in heaven? We find the answer in 1 Timothy 6:17-19 *"Command those who are rich in this present world not to be arrogant nor to put their hope in wealth, which is so uncertain, but to put their hope in God, who richly provides us with everything for our enjoyment. Command them to do good, to be rich in good deeds, and to be generous and* *willing to share. **In this way they will LAY UP TREASURES FOR THEMSELVES** as a foundation for the coming age, so that they may take hold of the life that is truly life."* We see here that we lay up treasures for ourselves in heaven by using our wealth and riches to do good deeds for other people and to be generous and willing to share. Jesus told His disciples that even a cup of cold water given in his name would not go unrewarded. Let us remember that as we do good deeds here on earth, we are storing for ourselves treasures in heaven. The life that is truly life will be lived in heaven and not here on earth.

PRAYER

Heavenly Father, thank you for the warnings that you have given me in this chapter. Please forgive me for many times I have lived as though I will live here on earth forever. I have not striven to be rich towards you. Holy Spirit, help me remember that the life that I live here is temporary. One day my life will be required of me. Let me have used whatever wealth you give me to accomplish the purpose for which You sent me here on earth. Teach me how to store for myself treasures in heaven where thieves cannot break in and steal. Today I commit to relinquish all my wealth and riches to you. I want to be rich in good deeds and to be generous and willing to share, no matter how little I think that I have. I now take authority and command every spirit that is not of You to leave me now in the mighty name of Jesus! Spirits of **love of money, arrogance, stinginess, fear, greed, complacency, self-reliance, hoarding, covetousness, and selfishness** leave me now in the name of Jesus Christ! You have no place in me. Be gone in Jesus name! Breathe out through your mouth until you feel relief. You may feel sensations in your hands and feet. You may feel like yawning or coughing. Let the spirits leave you. He who the Son sets free is free indeed!

CHAPTER 13

SOWING ON STRANGE ALTARS

This chapter will address a subject that many people ignore. It pertains to giving money to witchdoctors and false prophets. Many Christians are not aware of what their grandparents and great grandparents did. Unknown to them, some of their forefathers went to see witchdoctors and medicine- men, and paid them for their services. Worshiping another god invites a curse from God! We see this principle in Deuteronomy 28:14. *" Do not turn aside from any of the commands I give you today, to the right or to the left, following other gods and serving them."* Witchdoctors serve another god and when we solicit their services we join them in serving another god! The Bible is very clear about the consequences of following another god. *"...all these curses will follow you and overtake you."* Proverbs 3:33 also says, *"The Lord's curse is on the house of the wicked, but he blesses the home of the righteous."* The Word of God describes going to see a witchdoctor as, wickedness.

The satanic powers that witchdoctors use come from the demonic altars that they raise. Every altar is sustained by sacrificing on it, and that is why these evil practitioners will always ask their clientele to bring chickens, sheep, goats etc. for sacrifice. Satan knows that a blood sacrifice forges a very strong covenant with him. Once the animal one brings is sacrificed, the person who brought the sacrifices is connected to that altar and that altar will begin to speak into the life of the person. In Revelation15:7 we hear an altar speaking. *"And I heard the altar respond: 'Yes Lord God Almighty, true and just are your judgments.'"* This was a godly altar and it praised God. However, an evil altar will speak evil into the lives of people connected with it.

In Numbers chapter 22 we see king Balak inviting a witchdoctor called Balaam to come and curse Israel for him. As soon as the witchdoctor arrived the first thing king Balak did was to raise an altar through sacrifice. *"Balak sacrificed cattle and sheep..."* – verse 40. As soon as blood was shed a demonic altar was raised against Israel. Although this altar was raised, it did not affect Israel. In fact anytime Balaam opened his mouth, only blessings flowed out! Then Balaam the witchdoctor said, *"How can I curse those whom God has not cursed?"* The reason why Balaam could not curse Israel was because God's people were not under God's curse by worshiping other gods. When I give my money to a witchdoctor, my money becomes connected to a strange altar. This strange altar will only speak poverty and lack over my life! One of the curses in Deuteronomy 28:29 says, *"You will be unsuccessful in everything you do."* A lot of people who come to our counselling offices often tell us how they had a particular stubborn problem and when they shared it with a friend, their friend suggested to them that they take them to see someone who could solve their problem. God warned the Israelites through the prophet Isaiah about this very situation. *"When men tell you to consult mediums and spiritists, who whisper and mutter, should not a people inquire of their God?"* – Isaiah 8:19.

In Western countries people may not go to see people called witchdoctors, but they will go to solicit the services of palm readers, clairvoyances and people who use strange powers to contact the demonic world. Many people who are members of secret societies like the Freemasons are connected to strange altars. When we give our money to anyone who uses demonic power, we have sown in a strange altar and we will reap the consequences. The unfortunate thing is that we do not reap alone. Deuteronomy 5:9 says, *"You shall not bow down to them or worship them; for I, the Lord your God, am a jealous God, punishing the children for the sin of the fathers to the third and fourth generation of those who hate me."* If my forefathers up to four generations back sowed in strange altars then it should not come as a surprise when I am undergoing financial difficulties.

FALSE PROPHETS

I believe that false prophets are more dangerous than witchdoctors. While it is possible for a Christian to avoid going to see a witchdoctor because it is such an obvious and blatant sin, many Christians have found themselves before a false prophet without meaning to. One such case concerns a church elder that came to see me. This person, let me call her Tabitha, worshipped in a well-established mainstream church. She was the kind of mature believer that I would have not expected to be deceived by a false prophet but unfortunately she was!

It all started when she was overlooked when other people at her office were given promotions. When this happened a second time, she got desperate and talked to a colleague, Martha (not her real name), about it. Martha confirmed that she had also noticed how Tabitha's boss seemed to hold something against her. Martha told Tabitha that she knew a man of God who could pray for her to resolve this unfair situation and stop the apparent persecution against her. Being a prayerful woman, this idea appealed to Tabitha, who thought that this was the right thing to do – Bring the situation before God. Tabitha and Martha decided on a day that they would go to see the man of God. On arrival Tabitha noticed that the

"Man of God" looked young, like he was a man in his late twenties. He introduced himself as Saif (not his real name), and asked Tabitha what the problem was. She said that all she wanted to do was pray concerning the situation at work. Saif brought out a basin and placed it in front of Tabitha then filled it with water. He asked her to look into the water, and she saw a hand written letter at the bottom of the basin. Saif proceeded to remove the dripping letter from the water and asked Tabitha to read it. The letter was supposedly, written by her boss asking a witchdoctor to kill Tabitha. He was also confirming in the letter that he had already sent the witchdoctor 10,000 Kenya shillings! Tabitha was understandably concerned. She asked Saif what she should do. He told her that they needed to cancel the spell from her boss' witchdoctor, and to do that she would need to pay double what her boss had paid. Tabitha said that she did not have 20,000 Kenya shillings with her. Saif told her that she could pay whatever amount she had and commit to pay the rest later. Tabitha gave Saif 5,000 Kenya shillings, promising to send him the rest of the money by the end of that week. Tabitha left Saif's house feeling uneasy and scared. As soon as she got to her house, she got a call from Saif reminding her to keep her promise! The next day Saif called again early in the morning but this time Tabitha did not answer the call. This continued for three days with Saif calling and Tabitha not responding. By the fourth day Tabitha was fearful at all times. She found herself constantly looking behind her as though there was someone following her. The phone calls from Saif continued. As fear set in, so did lack of sleep. By now Tabitha had realized that Saif was a false prophet but she did not know what to do. She condemned herself for having allowed herself to be deceived. Tabitha told me that after her meeting with Saif, she started losing money. It was during this terrible season of her life that Tabitha came to see me. She had sowed her money on a strange altar and had already started reaping the consequences. Tabitha confessed the sin of worshiping another god, prayed to renounce Saif's altar, broke the ungodly soul tie with that altar, asked Jesus to cleanse her with His blood then we commanded all the evils spirits that were oppressing her to leave in the name of Jesus Christ!

Jesus gave us a stern warning in Matthew chapter 7 that is worth reading. False prophets are not a recent phenomenon. *"Watch out for false prophets. They come to you in sheep's clothing but inwardly are ravenous wolves..."* How do we recognize false prophets? A false prophet will not point you to Jesus Christ, but to an enemy who is a person. Saif pointed Tabitha to her boss who he claimed was trying to kill her. They will ask for money in order for them to pray for you. They will not mention Jesus Christ but will keep talking about God. We have to ask ourselves which god he or she is talking about. Many false prophets will often ask you to bring something physical to aid in the prayer – candles, salt, cloth, oil, chicken, egg etc. Prayer is engaging God in conversation and does not require anything in order for God to hear us, except a humble and contrite spirit. Tabitha did not have to pay 20,000 Kenya shillings in order for Saif to pray and break the curse over her. The most unfortunate thing that happened to Tabitha was that Satan had a legal right to attack her finances since she had willingly taken it to his altar! It is possible for someone to use money that we have given, to go and see a witchdoctor. It is for that reason that whenever we give money to someone, we must exchange the ownership of that money and declare that it no longer belongs to us, but that it now belongs to the person to whom we have given that money.

Satan is portrayed as cunning and sly, and who can deceive the very elect if it were possible. It is for this very reason that Paul warns believers not to be unaware of his schemes!

PRAYER

Heavenly Father, I believe that You are the only One and true God. I have got no desire to worship any other god but You. Thank you for all that You have taught me in this chapter concerning sowing on a strange altar. Forgive me for sowing on a strange altar (take some time and confess specifically you if have ever gone to see a witchdoctor or a false prophet). If you are guilty, below is a prayer that you can pray:

"Father I come to You as the Righteous Judge, I stand accused by Satan for taking my money to a strange altar. Please forgive me for worshiping another god, and making myself, and my future generations liable to financial curses. I ask you Lord Jesus as my Advocate to wash me in Your precious blood! I renounce and denounce every demonic altar that is speaking over my life and especially my finances. I silence you in Jesus name! I now take authority and command every **spirit of witchcraft, occult, divination, sorcery, necromancy, astrology, Freemasonry, satanic rituals, charms, fetishes** and anything demonic to come out of me right now in the name of Jesus Christ! Out in Jesus name! You have no place in me. Be gone in Jesus name!" Breathe out through your mouth until you feel relief. You may feel sensations in your hands and feet. You may feel like yawning or coughing. Let the spirits leave you. He who the Son sets free is free indeed!

PRAYERS TO BREAK FINANCIAL CURSES

I would suggest that you take one day to fast before you bring these prayers before God. Fasting causes us to be humble before God and it shows Him that we are totally depending on Him. Fasting also crucifies the flesh thus strengthening the inner spirit, and causing us to hear God more clearly.

People long to break financial curses so that they can provide for themselves and their dependents. Poverty has never elevated anybody. Jesus died so that we would live abundant lives. As you have read this book there may have been some areas where the Holy Spirit is challenging you to repent and make a change. Do not ignore it. It may be one of the reasons why you are not living in financial freedom. The Bible says that the borrower is slave to the lender. Slavery is not our portion in Jesus name. As you pray, come in total faith that you are coming to the Lord of Lords and the Creator and Giver of all things!

PRAYER OF REPENTANCE

Lord Jesus, I believe you are the Son of God and that you died for my sins and rose again from the dead. You love me and have always wanted the best for me. The plans You have for me are for welfare and not for evil. Lord you know my problems and how I have suffered financially. Thank you for all you have taught me about financial curses. I believe that as I pray, I am receiving according to Mark 11:24.

I believe you are the Messiah who came in the flesh to destroy the works of the devil. You died on the Cross for my sins and rose again from the dead. I now confess all my sins and repent. I claim forgiveness and cleansing. I believe that your blood cleanses me now from all sin. Thank you for redeeming me, cleansing me, and justifying me in your blood. I confess to you my sins of idolatry such as witchcraft, occult, divination, sorcery, calling on dead ancestral spirits, loving the world and the things of the world above God. Lord, I also confess that I have not loved, but have resented certain people who hurt or disappointed me and have held un-forgiveness in my heart. I call upon You, Lord, to help me forgive them. I do now forgive (mention their names, both living and dead) and ask you to forgive them also and bless them, Lord. I also now forgive myself in the name of Jesus Christ. I also confess the stealing of other people's property, which has brought a curse of theft upon our lives (Zechariah 5:1-4). I declare that my property and the property of my descendants will not be stolen again.

Heavenly Father, I bow in worship and praise you. I cover myself with the blood of Jesus Christ as my protection. I surrender myself completely and unreservedly in every area of my life to you. I stand against all the work of Satan, which would hinder me in my prayer life and deliverance from financial curses. I address myself only to the true and living God and refuse any involvement with Satan in my prayer. Satan, I command you, in the name of the Lord Jesus Christ, to loose your hold from my finances! I bring the blood of Jesus Christ between us. I resist every effort of Satan and his wicked spirits to attack me financially. I pull down all the strongholds of Satan in the name of Jesus Christ!

I come to You Lord Jesus as my Deliverer. You know all my problems and all the things that have brought poverty, lack, and struggling in my life. I now loose my finances from every dark spirit, every evil influence, all satanic bondage, and from every spirit in me, which is not the Holy Spirit of the Living God. I command all such spirits to leave me now in the name of Jesus Christ. Through the blood of Jesus, I am redeemed out of the hand of the devil. Through the blood of Jesus all my sins are forgiven. The blood of Jesus Christ God's Son is cleansing me now from all sin. Through the blood of Jesus I am justified, made righteous, just as if I had never sinned. Through the blood of Jesus I am sanctified, made holy, set apart for God. My body is a temple for the Holy Spirit, redeemed, cleansed, sanctified – by the blood of Jesus. I belong to the Lord Jesus Christ, God's only Son – body, soul and spirit. His blood protects me from all evil. Because of the blood of Jesus, Satan has no more power over me. I renounce him and his hosts completely and declare them to be my enemies. In the mighty name of the Lord Jesus Christ, son of the Living God, I pray. AMEN!

BREAK THE CURSE

And now as a servant of the Living God, I take authority and break every curse over my finances from the fourth, third, second and first generation. I renounce and denounce all the activities of my forefathers that have release a curse of poverty and stagnation in my life! I renounce their shrines, satanic altars, dedications, spoken curses, broken promises and vow, satanic covenants oaths, libations, traditions blood sacrifices and incantations that connected me and my future generations to evil and dark satanic forces! I declare that my finances and wealth are set free from the control and manipulation of evil spirits! I am set free in the name of Jesus Christ! I declare that today _____(slot in today's day, month and year) every curse is broken over my finances in the name of Jesus Christ! – AMEN!

PETITIONS

(The petitions below have been put together by Kaanan Ministries in South Africa)

- Father, in the name of Jesus Christ of Nazareth, I petition for my finances on behalf of myself and my ancestors. I confess the withholding of tithes and offerings, the love of money, gambling, bribery, fraud and all forms of stealing. I cancel all worship given to Baal and Mammon through these sins. I ask that you will break the curse that this has brought upon us and change it into a blessing for me, and my descendants. I cut my finances lose from the goddess of luck.

- I petition against all defilement of seed where finances were paid into the kingdom of Satan and used for his purposes. I petition for the cleansing and sanctification of this seed by the blood of Jesus and that this seed may be redeemed back into the kingdom of Jesus Christ! I declare every curse against my finances broken and changed into a blessing in the name of Jesus Christ.
- I petition against the dragon appointed over my treasure chest, whether in the heavens, on the earth, below the earth or in the waters in the name of Jesus Christ.
- I petition against every bird that has been sent out to peck up my seed. I ask Father that you throw out Your nets of fire and brimstone according to Ps. 11:6 over these birds.
- I petition that all finances that belong to my ancestors and that are locked up in the underworld be released and returned to the Kingdom of Jesus Christ. I petition that all finances that belong to my ancestors and that were not claimed, be returned to me now in the name of the Lord Jesus Christ. I also petition that all finances stolen from my ancestors and me be repaid sevenfold in the name of Jesus Christ of Nazareth.
- I petition against every snake that has been sent out to swallow my seed. I command every snake to spit out my seed in the name of Jesus Christ. I ask Father that you will cleanse and sanctify my seed with the blood of Jesus Christ of Nazareth.
- In the name of Jesus I now cut my finances loose from all the satanic financial world systems, Freemasons, every Secret Society, the "Grim Reaper", Satanic pests, and Satanic locusts.
- In the name of Jesus Christ of Nazareth I break the seasons of poverty, hunger and drought over my life. I break all curses of poverty, shortages, bankruptcy and barrenness over me. I bind every spirit assigned to these curses and strip them of

their power and authority and command them to become the footstool of Jesus Christ.

- I now petition before Your throne that You will open the windows of heaven over me according to Your word in Malachi 3, and pour out Your blessings in abundance, from your treasure chambers. I petition before Your throne that blessings, prosperity and favour will begin to rain upon me.

- I petition that the time- clock of Satan over my finances be destroyed with fire of the Holy Ghost and I ask that the time clock of Jesus Christ will become activated over my finances.

- I petition that my finances and harvests will be dedicated to Jesus Christ from now on.

- I prophesy that the season is changing over my finances. I declare that the season of Jesus Christ has begun over every area of my life!

- I bring all the wounds that I have received in my life due to finances before You and I petition for Your healing balm, anointing and authority to be placed over these wounds and that it shall be a sign in the spirit that the price has been paid.

- I now place my finances under the Lordship of Jesus Christ of Nazareth. I dedicate it to You, Lord, and ask that you will give me wisdom to apply it correctly in Your Kingdom, the Kingdom of Jesus Christ.

- I now petition Father, that You give me the ability to make wealth. Give me wisdom, perseverance, courage, strength and the ability to see opportunities.

Thank you Father that You approve of these petitions on the basis of what Jesus did on the cross of Calvary. Now take some time and thank God for breaking your financial curse.

Matthew 24:28 tells us that, **"Wherever there is a carcass, there the vultures will gather."** A curse on an individual is like a carcass (dead and smelly creature) and the vultures can be equated to evil spirits. If you want to get rid of the vultures you first have to get rid of the carcass that attracted them in the first place. After you remove the carcass, the vultures will still be hovering over the place where the carcass was. You now have to chase the vultures away. The vultures will not come back so long as there is no carcass. Now that you have dealt with the curse, you now need to kick out (chase away) the evil spirits. Luke 10:19 tells us that Jesus has given us the authority to tread on snakes and scorpions (evil spirits) and to overcome all the power of the enemy! So now stand on the power and authority and kick out all the evil spirits!

I now take authority in the name of Jesus Christ and command all these evil spirits to leave me now. Depart from me in Jesus name! Breathe out after every spirit. Spirit of:

Mind control	Persecution	Anxiety
Fear	Unfairness	Rejection
Paranoia	Worry	Fear of rejection
Self- rejection	Fear of failure	Criticism
Insecurity	No fear of God	Faultfinding
Doubt	Stagnation	Judgmental
Skepticism	Unemployment	Dishonesty
Lack of faith	Joblessness	Dishonor of God
Theft	Vagabond	Dishonor of parents
Stealing	No property	Deception
Fraud	No promotion	Lying
Corruption	No progress	Witchcraft
Bribery	No favor	Spoken curse
Betting	No salary	Stingy
Debt	No rent	Mean
Not paying loans	Broke	Indifference

Not paying taxes	Not tithing	Passivity
Greed	Trust in man	Addictions
Covetousness	Material lust	Alcoholism
Irresponsible spending	Selfishness	Drugs
No savings	Self- condemnation	Nicotine
False Promises	Self- hatred	Laziness
Borrowing	Rebellion	Fatigue
Purse with holes	Anti- submissiveness	Tiredness
Poverty	Stubbornness	Depression
Lack	Guilt	Impatience
Struggling	Withdrawal	Infirmity
Failure	Isolation	Sickness

Thank you Jesus for setting me free! Today, _____
(day, date and year) I am set free and he/she who the Son sets free
is free indeed!

PRAYER FOR SALVATION

If you who are reading this book does not know Jesus Christ as your
Lord and Savior, then I have a message for you. You do not have
to continue struggling through the trials and hardships of life on
your own. God wants you to live a victorious life. Acts 4:12 tells us
that *"Salvation is found in no one else, for there is no other name
under heaven given among men by which we must be saved."* You
can make a decision today to begin a new life with Jesus by believing
in Him, and asking Him to forgive your sins. Salvation means giving
Jesus complete control over your life. It means turning away from a
life of sin and turning to God through repentance and letting Him
cloth you with His holiness.

Find a place to get down on your knees and pray:

> *"Father God I come to you today in the precious name of Jesus Christ, Your Son who died for me on the cross for my sins. Your word says, that everyone has sinned and fallen short of Your glory. The price for sin is death, but Your gift is eternal life. I confess that I have controlled my own life, which has been a life of sin. Please forgive me and cleanse me with the blood of Jesus. I ask you from today to accept me as your child. I ask you to take total control of my life as my Lord and Savior. Make me your child and write my name in the Book of Life. Help me live a life that is pleasing to you. I ask all this believing in the name of Jesus Christ – Amen!"*

If you have prayed this prayer and meant it from the bottom of your heart, then please find a Christian and tell them of this very important decision that you have made. Find a Bible–believing church where you can fellowship with other believers. Go up to the pastor and tell him that you have recently made a decision to follow Jesus Christ. If possible, join a small Bible study group where you can learn how to conduct your life according to the word of God. Remember that if a baby is born and not taken care of, he or she will die! Babies need milk, which is like the word of God for a believer. There are many devotional books that you can find from a Christian bookstore. Use it to guide you as you read the Bible. God bless you!

About the Author

Pastor Nellie Shani, a Kenyan who has been a Christian for over forty years, is Founder and CEO of Breaking Barriers International (BBI), a non-profit organization whose mission is to equip believers in Jesus Christ to live victoriously and fulfill their purpose in the world. She has adhered to this mission through her regular teachings on spiritual warfare and deliverance. Her deep revelations of the Word of God, is taught with clarity and simplicity. Besides being an author of seven books, she is also a conference speaker, preacher of the Word, and workshop leader. Pastor Nellie has been used by God to teach and train believers in the area of her calling in Africa, the United States of America, the United Kingdom, and Eastern Europe.

As a happily married woman to Dan Ole Shani, she has three grown children and two grandchildren. She draws much of her knowledge and experience from having lived with her family in six different countries, on three continents.

Other Books by Author

STAND YOUR GROUND

Many Christians live a life of defeat, harassed and bombarded by their arch enemy, Satan. They have not yet fully grasped that when Jesus Christ died on the cross, he completely and utterly defeated Satan!

He took back the authority Satan used to deceive Adam and Eve, handing it to the Church. However, our strength is of no use if we don't know we possess it!

This is the tragedy of our Lack of Knowledge.

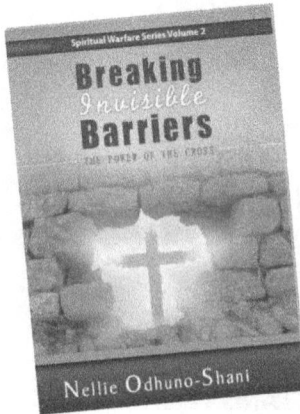

BREAKING INVISIBLE BARRIERS

Many Christians today are living a life of constant struggle and failure no matter what they do to try and improve their lot in life. They are fighting something they do not understand.

This book explores these invisible barriers and how to break them by the Power of the Cross.

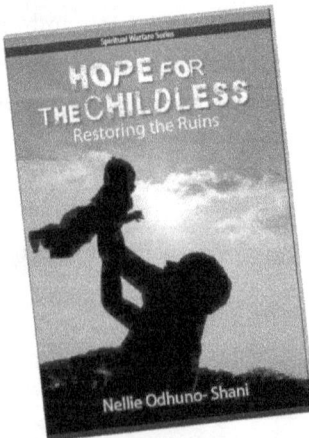

HOPE FOR THE CHILDLESS

God designed that every womb He has created be fruitful. Why then do we have people who cannot have children?

This book answers this question and shares the experiences of women who were not able to conceive or carry babies to full term, but today are mothers by the grace of God.

STEP INTO SUPERNATURAL POWER

Although the Holy Spirit is present and busy in the whole Bible, He is often relegated to the New Testament and more specifically, to the Book of Acts after the Day of Pentecost. What was the Holy Spirit's role in the Old Testament? How is He recognised in the life of a believer? Is His presence IN a believer the same as His presence UPON a believer? Is speaking in tongues really necessary? This book on spiritual warfare emphasises the role of the Holy Spirit in the Old and New testaments.

WHEN TWO HALVES MAKE A HOLE

Behind every broken marriage is a fierce battle that was lost in the spiritual realm. Many people do not realise that from the moment they say "I do" a raging battle starts whose sole objective is the break-up of their marriage. The Bible warns us that our enemy the devil prowls around like a roaring Lion looking for someone to devour. We are told not to be passive a onlooker but to "Resist him..." Thus the battle for our marriage is not an option but a command.

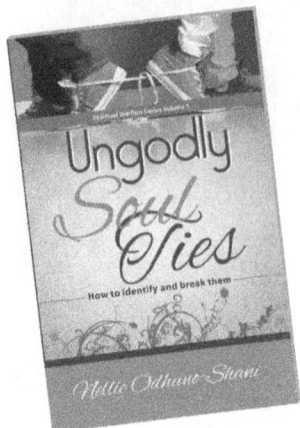

UNGODLY SOUL TIES

Did you know that there are relationships that we walked away from as many as ten years ago that can still keep us in bondage? Many people are not aware that the way they behave today may be directly related to the way their parents, or even a kindergarten teacher treated them in childhood. Ungodly soul ties are often forged between us by people who have abused us physically, emotionally or psychologically. This book will tell you how to identify and break them through the power of the cross of Jesus Christ.